FANTASTIC FACTS!

JOHN MAY

Foreword by Jonathan Ross

CARLTON

BLOOMSBURY

First published in Great Britain 1993

Copyright © Carlton Television Ltd
Channel X Ltd and Carlton Books Ltd 1993

Bloomsbury Publishing Ltd
2 Soho Square, London W1V 5DE

ISBN 0 7475 1573 5

10 9 8 7 6 5 4 3 2 1

Pictures supplied by Carlton Television, Popperfoto and Rex Features

Cover photographs: (*front*) John Brown; (*back*) John Brown,
Pat Dyos and Ken Loveday.

Printed and bound in Great Britain by Bath Press

CONTENTS

ACKNOWLEDGEMENTS

It is a pleasure to have the opportunity to thank the many people who have made *Fantastic Facts!* a reality.

First and foremost, to my friend and collaborator Kim Fuller, whose belief in the project kept the idea alive through all the difficulties.

Secondly, to Jonathan Ross, the main man, whose sheer professionalism, graciousness and enthusiasm were greatly appreciated.

Many thanks are due to the team Channel X assembled to produce the TV series on which this book is based: to the top team of Alan Marke, Heather Hampson, Kenton Allen and Ian Hamilton; to those fearless researchers Cillian de Buitlear, Howie Jaffe, Lucy Robinson, Katie Taylor, Belinda Harris and John Fitzgerald; to writers Victoria Pile and Jez Stevenson; the unflappable and indispensable Meena Sud; to that wizard set designer Colin Pigott and his assistant Danae Yamalaki; to the location crew of Mark Linsey, Andrew Gillman and Pippa Haddow; to the valuable production team of Angie Hill and Anna Staniland; to that master of the floor Mike Morgan, to those tireless runners Ian Coyle and Natasha Lewis, to those inventive animators Martin Poole, Andrew Godden and Stuart Rideout of Original Graphics and to the many others (thanks Miles for getting us started) who helped bring *Fantastic Facts!* to the screen.

The many guests who appeared in the series demonstrated that the world is truly a remarkable place. Hats off in particular to Wilf Lunn, the Rev Howard and Robert Haag.

My personal thanks are due to my agent Rachel Daniels for her perseverance and to Mark Berlin for his wise advice.

Thanks also to the team at Carlton Books, Jonathan Goodman, Piers Murray Hill and my editor Martin Corteel, and to John Bishop at Carlton Television.

This book is dedicated specially to you Louis, with all my love.

JM
Lewes
26 January 1993

INTRODUCTORY WARNING from Jonathan Ross

This book contains stories, reports and pieces of information so ridiculous, outlandish and, quite frankly, unbelievable, that they will make you cry out in disbelief. 'Impossible! No way! They must be joking! There are some very sick minds at work here!' Exclamations like these could prove very embarrassing if they flew from your lips while browsing through **Fantastic Facts!** on the bus or train, or even in your classroom during a particularly boring lesson.

Therefore, heed this warning. Keep your mouth tightly shut when you read, with wonder, about the fainting goats. Try your hardest to resist gasping too loud at the true but pathetic story of the bat-bombs. Keep schtum when you get to the bit about Kin and Gin, the world's oldest pop stars. Try, if you can, to avoid nudging your neighbour too hard in the ribs when you encounter the ridiculous but true saga of 'The Regurgitator', a man who travels the world getting paid to swallow things and bring them back up again. Because, despite what any sane person might think, all the items contained herein are 100 per cent, no ifs or buts, believe it or not, TRUE. They are *Facts* and what's more, they are all **Fantastic** ones. Which is how, incredible as it might seem, we came up with the title for the television series that spawned this beautiful tome.

I must admit, when I came across some of the gems collected here for the first time, I too was sceptical. Before committing myself to the project I enlisted the aid of the most up-to-the-minute computer technology, gained access to the largest information database and, in a final desperate bid to prove their authenticity, I collected every story in the book into a huge pile and waved a small magic wand that had been given to me by the popular children's entertainer, Sooty. Finally, I declared myself satisfied. I can confidently assure you that this book contains nothing but facts ... facts that have <u>earned</u> the title **Fantastic.** If they weren't, of course, then they would have no business being in this book. Let's be honest, a collection entitled *Quite Interesting Facts*, or *Mildly Unusual Facts* would have been of very little interest to anyone.

So, prepare to be amazed, amused, delighted, confounded, astounded, dumbfounded and tickled by the most incredible collection of strange but true knick-knacks I have ever written an introduction for. And remember, everything in this book is TRUE. Trust me, I'm a television presenter.

P.S. Everything except the bit about the magic wand. That's a teeny exaggeration.

7

FANTASTIC PEOPLE!

MEMORY MEN

Creighton Herbert James Carvello, a psychiatric nurse from Middlesborough, recited by heart the value of *pi* to 20,013 places in nine hours, ten minutes. (He subsequently lost this world-record to Hideaki Tomoyori of Japan, who reached 40,000 places).

He subsequently memorised his local phone book and can also name every player who has been in a FA Cup Final since the event began more than a century ago.

SAVANTS

'Idiot Savants', like the Dustin Hoffman character in the movie *Rain Man*, suffer from autism a mysterious disabling disease which leaves them unable to communicate normally. As a result, they withdraw into a private world. Ten per cent of the 7,500 children world-wide who suffer from autism develop extra-ordinary talents as a result.

★　★　★

Savants' skills can be categorised as follows: calendar calculation, artistic talent, mechanical dexterity, musical ability, unusual mathematical skills, memorising obscure facts and the ability to identify substances of all kinds by their smell.

★　★　★

Famous 'idiot savants' include the following:

✪ J.H. Pullen, known as 'the genius of Earlswood Asylum' until his death in 1918. He built a three metre (10 ft) -long highly detailed scale model of the Great Eastern, his only guide being a picture of the ship on a handkerchief. He had to make one and a quarter million wooden pins to fasten the deck planks down.

✪ Blind Tom, a black slave born in Georgia in 1849. He could only communicate in grunts but could repeat – word for word – conversations in Italian, French and English. He also knew by heart 5,000 piano pieces.

✪ A boy called Robert, who lives on New York's Staten Island, can play eleven musical instruments by ear. He can also name the day of the week on any given date, back to 1937, and the correct date for any given day.

LIGHTNING CALCULATOR

Shakuntala Devi has been a mathematical prodigy since the age of three and gave her first public display when she was six. She earned the title 'world's fastest human computer' for working out the cube root of 2,37,927,704 in her head in 10 seconds.

In her book *Figuring* she writes: 'All along I cherished a desire to show those who think mathematics are dull and boring just how beautiful it can be.'

TALLIES

Phillip Heinricy is two metres (6 ft 8 in) tall and founder of the Tall Persons Club of Great Britain; He calls its 1400 members "tallies".

Twenty five per cent of the adult male population of Britain is now 1.8 m (6 ft) or over. The height of the average Briton has increased ten centimetres (4 ins) since 1860 but the length of the standard size British bed has not changed at all in the same period.

KIN & GIN

Japan's celebrated 100 year-old twins stand 1.2 m (4 ft 1 in) tall, weigh 32 kg (70 lb) and have five teeth between them, yet their CD *Kin-chan to Gin-chan* sold more than 100,000 copies. They have also starred in a tv soap opera, a chat show and a commercial for Duskin, a manufacturer of dusters and kitchen towels. (The link is the fact that the company's telephone number is 100-100).

Both Kin & Gin their names mean gold and silver respectively – are widowed great-grandmothers, born on 1 August 1892. In Japan, a long life is considered an honour. Many children will be named after them.

Japanese women have the longest life-expectancy in the world (eighty-two years) with men not far behind (seventy-six). As Japan also has one of the lowest birth-rates in the world, it population is rapidly greying. This explains the lively centenarians' popularity.

MASS-MARRIAGES

Followers of the Rev. Sun Myung Moon, founder of the Unification Church get married at mass-weddings. In 1992, twenty thousand brides and grooms were wed in the Olympic Stadium in Seoul, the capital of South Korea. A further 10,000 couples from five countries were linked into the ceremony via satellite tv link-up. Each couple paid a fee, generating ten million pounds for the church's funds.

The grooms were all dressed in identical suits and red ties; the brides

 This was a wet, rather than white, wedding. Sadly, the first problem came when the groom was told that he could kiss the bride.

in identical gowns, wearing identical veils and carrying identical bouquets.

Most of the couples had only just met each other and many could not even speak each other's languages. They had been personally matched by the Rev Moon using photos and a computer.

There are no mass-honeymoons after the event. Church rules forbid sex until forty days after the wedding.

MOST MARRIED WOMAN

Linda Essex has been married and divorced more times than any other woman. She married fifteen different men, five of them twice and one of them three times. The longest marriage lasted seven years, the shortest thirty hours. By the time you read this, she may be married again.

SKYDIVING DIVORCE

Lynda and Gene Ballard ended their sixteen-year marriage by staging a skydiving divorce, 3,048 m (10,000 ft) above Antioch, California, with the help of their lawyer and six of their closest friends. Lynda was a veteran of 750 parachute jumps and her husband had made 1,800 skydives. 'Almost everything in our marriage was done around skydiving, ' said Lynda, 'so the divorce in the air seemed the natural thing to do.'

DECREE NISI

In a divorce case in Germany, the wife revealed that her husband only spoke an average of three words a day to her. In over two months he managed just twenty-six sentences. When he did speak, his words were less than complementary. 'This coffee tastes like washing-up' was one choice offering.

UNUSUAL MUSICIANS

Derek Paravicini made his London concert debut in July 1989 at the Barbican in London, with the Royal Philharmonic Orchestra. At the time, he was nine years old and had a mental age of six. He has been totally blind since birth.

Evelyn Glennie is much in demand as a soloist and orchestral player on percussion. Evelyn has been 'profoundly' deaf since she was twelve. She stays in sync with an orchestra by following the score, 'feeling' the vibrations of the music and observing what's going on around her. With a pianist, she watches the foot pedals and facial movements and other clues she can get.

MODERN MUMMIES

For an asking price of around $31,000, John Chew and his colleagues at the Summum Corporation of Salt Lake City, Utah will preserve you 'indefinitely' through a process of modern mummification.

The technique they use is as follows. The body is first soaked in a secret patented mixture of chemical preservatives, herbs and white wine for two months. (Red wine discolours the skin). The body is then dried and treated with oils and lotions to keep the skin smooth and supple, forever. It is then wrapped in linen gauze and coated with polyurethane or latex rubber and put inside a fibreglass casting. It is finally welded into a sarcophagus moulded into the shape of the human form, called a 'mummiform', and the inert gas, argon is used to remove any oxygen inside. The purging holes are then sealed and it is ready for installation in the mausoleum of your choice.

The mummification process costs from $7,500-11,000; the mummiforms from $24,000 to one million dollars plus, depending on how elaborate they are.

More than 140 people, including a number of famous celebrities, have signed up for mummification to date but, as they are mainly aged between thirty-five and fifty-five, no-one has yet been through the process.

Kay Henry, a Salt Lake City talk show host is one of their clients. She wants to have her mummiform inlaid with a microphone and wants to take her tv, CD player and stuffed animals with her. One man has ordered his in the shape of an Oscar statuette.

The Summum Corporation, which began business producing wines, known as 'nectar publications' – essential for mummification – in a pyramidal winery, now have plans to construct a giant granite vault in a Utah mountain range, big enough to hold 800 mummiforms.

CROMWELL'S HEAD

One thing they never tell you in history at school is that Oliver Cromwell's head led a 'life' after its body was dead.

Cromwell died on 3 September 1658, of an infection caused by a stone in the bladder and was already buried by the time a state funeral was staged in his honour two months later.

The Royalists were still seeking revenge for the killing of King Charles and, by order of Parliament in January 1661, Cromwell's body and those of two of his closest henchmen were exhumed. Two of the corpses (the other had rotted away) were taken to the gibbet at Tyburn – on the site of the modern-day Marble Arch in London – and hung from the gallows for a day.

The bodies were then beheaded and the heads stuck on iron poles outside Westminster Hall.

The story goes that they stayed there until about 1684 when a fierce gale finally dislodged Cromwell's head which landed at a sentry's feet. He wrapped it in his cloak and took it home where he hid it in a chimney for the rest of his life, only revealing its existence to his family on his deathbed.

The head subsequently passed through the hands of many individuals and was widely exhibited as a curiosity.

A thorough scientific examination was carried out on the head in the 1930s by two cranial detectives who became convinced of its authenticity. There was even a brown spot on the parchment-like skin, corresponding to Cromwell's distinctive wart.

The head was finally laid to rest on 25 March 1960 in the ante chapel of Sydney Sussex College in Cambridge, where Cromwell had been a student. It was buried in an oak box with a red silk lining.

GROOVER

Dr Arthur Lintgen has an unusual talent. He can name any classical record by just looking at its grooves. He gains clues from the shape and closeness of the grooves, from the construction of the album and the length of each track.

DESERT CURATE

In 1975, the Reverend Geoffrey Howard, a parish priest from Manchester, pushed a wheelbarrow across the Sahara from Beni Abbes in Algeria to Kano in Nigeria, a distance of 3,220 km (2,000 miles) which he covered in ninety-three days.

He was the first man to cross the Sahara on foot, unaided by a vehicle or camel and using only natural supplies and watering points.

His vehicle was an ancient Chinese sailing wheelbarrow, designed to catch the trade winds that blow across the Sahara and ideal for carrying his camping gear, water, food and medical supplies. The Rev Howard aimed not only to prove the value of this vehicle as the best man-powered machine for transporting heavy loads over soft or rough terrain but also to test his own faith. He also raised money for charity through this unusual expedition.

During the trek, he was backed up by a British Army team of two men with a Land Rover, but they were only allowed to give him fresh stocks of food and water at agreed points

UEMURA

The first man to reach the North Pole, solo, after a fifty-seven-day, 725-km (450-mile) journey, in temperatures of – 22 °C (-7 °F), was thirty-seven year-old Naomi Uemura, in 1978.

He faced exceptional problems right from the beginning of his journey from Canada's remote Ellesmere Island. For a start, more than one hundred of his huskies suffocated to death in their crates when being flown in.

Uemura set off with nineteen dogs for the final run to the Pole. Four days out, he was attacked by a polar bear which destroyed his tent and devoured the huskies' food. He fought it off but it returned the next night, forcing him to kill it with a rifle shot at seventy metres (225 ft). He fed the meat to the dogs.

Uemura suffered severe facial frostbite and the pressure ridges on the ice – up to nine metres (30 ft) high – meant that he had to detour and back-track constantly to make any progress. He battled against loneliness by keeping a diary for a Japanese literary magazine, which helped to pay the $400,000 cost of the expedition.

The sixth, and youngest child of a mat-maker, Uemura began exploring to overcome an inferiority complex. He became the first man to climb the highest summits in five continents and also sailed 6,500 km (4,000 miles) up the Amazon river on a balsa wood raft.

Uemura was reported missing, presumed lost, in April 1984, after making the first solo winter ascent of Mt McKinley in Alaska.

SURVIVORS

A confectionery salesman from Kent won a thirty-five minute battle for his life when his car landed upside down in 1.5 m (5 ft) of water. It took him ten minutes to force his way into the car's trunk, five minutes to clear away his samples and find a wrench, and fifteen minutes of hammering before the lock gave way, leaving him enough room to squeeze out to the surface.

He recalls: 'It was really a halfpenny which saved my life. It was the only coin I had in my pocket and I used it to unscrew the back seat to get into the boot...As I worked on the screws I could feel the water collecting underneath me on the roof. I worked away at the lock of the boot..It was the only chance I had. Finally it gave, but as soon as I moved the boot lid, the water and mud gushed in.'

A US army sergeant fell 335 m (1,100 ft) when his parachute failed to open over West Virginia and his reserve chute became tangled. He landed on his feet, rolled on his back and suffered only a cracked vertebrae.

ECCENTRICS

Eccentrics are 'exceptional individuals with insight into the differentness,' according to an American psychiatrist, Dr David Weeks at the Royal Edinburgh Hospital, who has made a five-year study of the subject.

He advertised widely for eccentrics to get in touch with him and was rewarded by meeting a man who lives in cave that is partly submerged at low tide, a long-distance tricyclist, a pacifist who lives in a bombed-out house on the outskirts of Belfast, and a man who raises money for renal dialysis equipment by abseiling down tower blocks, dressed as a pink elephant.

There was also a man who refused to eat anything but potatoes, and an aristocratic woman who shared her home with thirty stuffed animals and kept a yellow plastic crab and red plastic lobster as pets, wheeling them around with her.

Dr Weeks concluded that eccentricity was the key to happiness and longevity. He has also studied eccentrics in the US and concludes that those in Britain are of a 'higher quality'. One Briton in 10,000 is eccentric, compared with one American in 15,000.

MAURICE SEDDON

Captain Seddon started his one-man electronics business, Audiogram, in 1957 after twelve years in the Royal Signals. His obsession with motorbikes and electronics led to him developing electrically-heated motorcycle-wear and then to an entire wardrobe of electrically-heated clothes, all based on the principle of the electric blanket.

His cottage has sockets all over the house, linked to a thirty-foot windmill in the garden, so that he can plug himself in as he moves from room to room.

Most of the ground floor of the house is taken up by a private museum of electronic antiques.

When travelling, he rides his ancient BSA B33 motorbike festooned with wires and cables that carries a modified alternator from a Mercedes to run his electrically heated gloves and suit.

BEACHCOMBER

Cornelius Ellen lives on the Frisian island of Texel, a twenty-six-kilometre (16-mile)-long sandy island which, during the winter, receives more than its fair share of the flotsam and jetsam floating in the North Sea.

'Cor', as he is known to the locals, has spent his life scanning the dunes, has furnished his house with what he's found and now part of his collection is in the local museum.

His first major find, in 1938 at the age of twelve, was a long leather cylinder, stamped with a British naval crest, that contained explosive.

Since then he has recovered from the sea: three years' supply of powdered milk; a message in bottle, thrown in the sea in 1950 by an English woman with whom Cor still corresponds; the engine of a Germany wartime Dornier bomber wrapped in a fisherman's net; and a page from the notebook of the purser on the great liner, *Queen Mary*.

HOBOS

Hobos are not tramps or winos but itinerant workers. That is the original sense of the word, at least – but where the word comes from is a matter of dispute.

It could come: from the name for migratory farm hands (hoe boys); from the French musical instrument used by wandering minstrels (*hautbois*, later hautboy then oboe); from the warning cry of the French Canadian lumberjacks ('*Haut bois*' – High timber!) or from the shouts of American railroad workers unloading mailbags ('Ho, boy!').

The celebrated King of the Hobos was 'Steam Train', Maury Graham, elected and crowned five times at the annual Hobo convention in Britt, Iowa. Graham rode the rails from the time he was fourteen in 1931 until 1980. According to him, the rail lines have been cut back so much that there may be no more than three hundred true hobos left.

HERMITS

Stefan Pietroszys, aged eighty-one, and his wife, aged sixty-one, lived for twenty eight years as hermits in a cave near a suburb of Sydney. They survived by eating berries, roots and mice.

According to Major Ivan Uncomb of the Salvation Army, the couple emigrated to Australia after World War II and went into hiding because they thought Soviet KGB agents were chasing them. The husband was taken into a hostel when his wife died in February 1979.

HITLER

Not a single personal letter of Hitler's exists. During his last days, in his twenty-room bunker in Berlin, all of Hitler's documents had to be typed out for him in letters three times normal size on special 'Fuhrer typewriters'.

Hitler did not swim and never got in a rowing boat or mounted a horse.

HUMAN PHENOMENA

Tripp and Bowen were a famous double-act at the music halls. Tripp had no arms and Bowen had no legs. They used to ride a tandem bicycle together with Tripp saying 'Bowen, watch your step', and Bowen replying: 'Keep your hands off me.'

James Morris had 'elastic skin'. He could pull the skin of his chest up to the top of his head and stretch his cheeks eight inches out from the side of his face.

Among Barnum and Bailey's Giant American Museum of Human Phenomena and Prodigies, were the following: the Poodle Man, who had long silky hair covering his face, eyes, nose, ears, chin and neck; Alfonso, the Man with the Ostrich Stomach, who could chew up glass and pebbles, swallow nails, eat soap and wash it all down with gasoline and ammonia; the Telescope Man, a young American who had the ability to lengthen or shorten his spinal column at will, increasing and decreasing his height.

Mac Norton, the Human Aquarium, swallowed (and ejected) 13.63 litres (3 gal) of water and two dozen live frogs.

BEARDED LADY

Julia Pastrana was billed as the 'Ugliest Woman in the World'. Discovered among the Digger Indians of Mexico, she was exhibited in London in 1857, married her manager a man named Lent and gave birth to a hairy daughter. When she died, shortly after the birth, in Moscow in 1862, her body was embalmed by a certain Professor Suckaloff and exhibited by Lent in London.

Lent then searched the world for her doppelganger. He found Marie Bartels, re christened her Leonora Pastrana and presented her at fairs and circuses as Julia's sister. He married her too, making him the only man in history to have had two bearded brides. Lent went mad before he died but was successful enough to enable his widow to retire from show business and acquire another husband, twenty years her junior.

PEERS

At the time of writing, there are 1,212 peers in the United Kingdom, the only country which still allows peers to have a direct effect on the nation's laws, by correcting or delaying them.

Peers are exempt from jury service (along with undischarged bankrupts, convicted felons and lunatics) and cannot be arrested for a civil case for forty days before or after a meeting of parliament, which only leaves a few days in the middle of summer.

The Duke of Atholl is the only man in Britain permitted a private army, an hon-

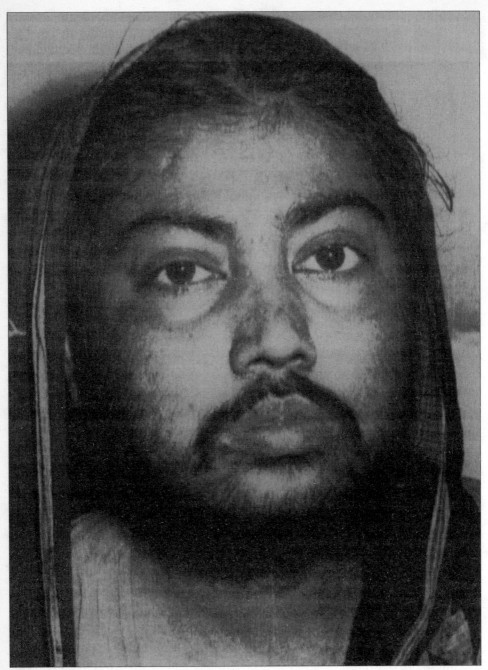

 FACT Shafia Khatun, a Bangladeshi, started to grow a beard when her menstrual cycle suddenly stopped when she was aged 34. She is now looking for a razor.

our awarded to his ancestors by Queen Victoria, against the wishes of the government of the day, in 1849.

The Duke of Buccleuch claims to be the only duke to have served, strictly incognito, on the lower deck of a destroyer during wartime, to have been elected four times to the Commons and to have escorted Ava Gardner. He owns more land than any other individual in Europe and is the owner of *The Madonna and the Yardwinder*, the only Leonardo da Vinci painting in private hands.

Lord Mansfield's only claim to fame was for prosecuting film star, Jayne Mansfield (no relation) for illegally importing ,'Momsicle' and 'Popsicle' , her two dogs, into the UK.

SAINTS

Legend has it that the youngest saint ever was St Rumwold, who died at the age of three. By this time she had, apparently, found her faith, asked for baptism and holy communion and even preached a sermon on the Holy Trinity.

St Sabine can be invoked against gout and rheumatism. St Apollonia against toothache, St Benedict Joseph Labre against contagious diseases, St Blase against sore throats and St Fiacre, the sixth century Irishman, against piles.

St Brigid of Ireland, the sixteenth century abbess of Kildare, allegedly transformed her used bath water into beer for visiting clerics.

There were two or possibly four St Valentines. The best known was a Roman priest in the third century AD, who was beaten and beheaded by Claudius the Goth. Two other Valentines were martyred, one in Africa and one in Rome.

Relics of the various St Valentines are scattered across Europe: there is a head in Italy, a body in Rome, two bodies and a head in Spain, two bodies in Belgium, and one body in Switzerland.

No-one knows how St Valentine acquired the reputation for protecting lovers.

PRESIDENTS

Gerald Ford was the only American president to have been a male model

Richard Nixon wore a steel-ribbed 'celebrity glove' to make handshaking easier during political campaigns.

Lyndon Johnson used to feed guests at his ranch with steaks cut into the shape of the State of Texas. He was also fond of making gifts of electric toothbrushes bearing the presidential seal. He claimed: 'I know that from now until the end of their days, they will think of me first thing in the morning and last at night.'

Jimmy Carter is the first US President to have been born in a hospital. All thirty-eight previous Presidents were born 'at home'.

Theodore Roosevelt was the first US President to ride in an automobile.

The first US President to be born in the twentieth century didn't take office until 1961 – John F. Kennedy. He was born in 1917.

Some extraordinary coincidences link the assassinations of Presidents Abraham Lincoln and John F. Kennedy.

✪ Both Presidents were concerned with the issue of civil rights.

✪ Lincoln was elected in 1860, Kennedy in 1960.

✪ Both Presidents were assassinated on a Friday and both in the presence of their wives.

✪ They were both shot from behind and in the head.

✪ Their successors, both named Johnson, were Southern Democrats and both were in the Senate.

✪ Andrew Johnson was born in 1808 and Lyndon Johnson in 1908

✪ Assassins John Wilkes Booth and Lee Harvey Oswald were Southerners favouring unpopular ideas.

✪ Booth and Oswald were both assassinated before it was possible for either of them to be brought to trial.

✪ Both Presidents' suffered the death of a child, while living in the White House.

✪ Lincoln's secretary, whose name was Kennedy, advised him not to go to the theatre.

✪ Kennedy's secretary, whose name was Lincoln, advised him not to make the trip to Dallas.

✪ John Wilkes Booth shot Lincoln in a theatre box and afterwards ran to a warehouse.

✪ Oswald shot Kennedy from a warehouse and ran to a theatre

✪ The last names of both Presidents contain seven letters

✪ The names of both assassins contain fifteen letters.

ACTORS

Bob Hope once tried a career in amateur boxing under the name, Packy Ease.

Rock Hudson was originally called Roy Fitzgerald. He got his name from his agent Henry Wilson, who claimed: 'I named him after the Rock of Gibraltar and the Hudson River.'

W.C.Fields was so afraid of losing his cash, he used to open bank accounts whenever he found himself with loose change in his pocket. Among the pseudonyms he used were: Figley E. Whitesides, Aristotle Hoop, Ludovic Fishpond and Cholmondley Frampton-Blythe. Hundreds of these bank accounts are still open all over the US. Fields never made a list of them, so many might never be closed down.

Humphrey Bogart once said: 'In my first twenty-nine pictures, I was shot in twelve, electrocuted or hanged in eight, and was a jailbird in nine. Is that a record to be proud of ?'

That is not James Dean's voice you hear in the drunken banquet scene in 'Giant'. The voice belongs to actor Nick Adams, who was paid $300 for three-days' dubbing. This was necessary because Dean's mumbling was inaudible; by the time the film was ready for re-dubbing, Dean was already dead and buried.

Peter Finch, the only actor to win an Oscar posthumously for his part in the movie 'Network', was the son of physicist Professor George Finch, who was a mountaineer on the 1922 Leigh-Mallory expedition to Mt Everest.

 Three masters of the horror movie genre share the same birthday: Peter Cushing (*top*), Christopher Lee (*below left*) and Vincent Price (*below right*) were all born on 27 May but in different years.

Horror movie stars, Peter Cushing, Vincent Price and Christopher Lee were all born on 27 May, though in different years.

Fidel Castro used was a film extra in Hollywood before becoming politically active. He appeared in such films as 'Bathing Beauties' with Esther Williams. According to band leader Xavier Cugat: 'He was a young, attractive, ambitious boy...and he had aspirations for being discovered. He was a typical Latin looker, so he was in quite a lot of crowd scenes in those big splashy films.' Cugat also claims he was a 'complete ham'.

Christopher Lee was Ian Fleming's cousin. Ian Fleming wanted Trevor Howard or Michael Redgrave to play the part of James Bond.

No actor has been portrayed on the screen by other actors more often than Charlie Chaplin.

David Niven began his film career as an extra, registered at Central Casting as 'Anglo Saxon type 2008'. His first role was as a Mexican in a blanket in a Hopalong Cassidy film. He was subsequently an extra in twenty-six other westerns.

The shortest adult-performer in the history of the movies was eighty centimetre (2 ft 7 in) tall, Tamara de Treaux, an actress and singer from San Francisco, who was one of three actors and actresses who played E.T. in the sections of the film that did not use an electronic puppet.

Lon Chaney, the greatest horror star of the silent cinema and a master of disguise, was born on 1 April 1883 to deaf and dumb parents. Among the enormous gallery of grotesque roles he played were vampires, phantoms, hunchbacks, clowns and a crooked ventriloquist.

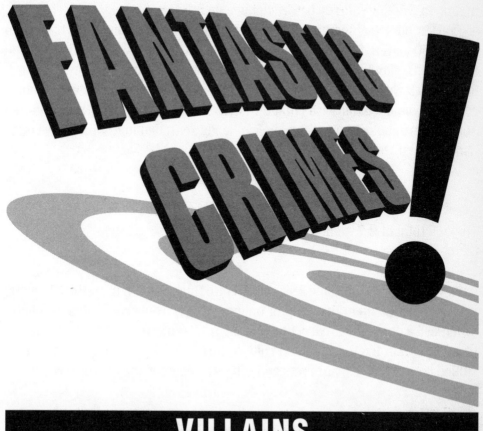

VILLAINS

Monk Eastman, a Brooklyn villain of the nineteenth century, cracked so many heads with his bludgeon that ambulance men renamed the accident ward of the local hospital, 'Eastman Pavilion.

French gangster, Jean-Charles Willoquet was arrested by members of The Anti-Gang Squad, an elite French police unit, while he was watching a program on tv about The Anti Gang Squad.

HOTEL THEFT

A forty-eight year old cleaner stole more than £13,000-worth of goods from a hotel in Dorking, Surrey before being caught.

Her haul included: thirteen coffee percolators, forty-one bathroom mugs, 350 knives, forks and spoons, ten kettles, five crystal chandeliers, 236 sheets, 180 pillow cases, 426 towels and tea towels, sixty ashtrays, 283 toilet rolls, a lavatory seat, a folding bed, cut glass, antiques, brassware, books.

The amazing thing was that during this four-year stealing spree, no-one noticed anything missing. When police finally searched her home, everything was neatly stored away unused.

Every twelve seconds, someone in America steals a towel from a Holiday Inn. That's a total of 2.7 million towels a year.

A survey by the Automobile Association into things stolen from British hotels in 1991 included an entire crop of onions (stolen from the garden of a hotel in Jersey), a dance-floor carpet measuring 6 x 3.6 metres (20 ft x 12 ft), stolen from a hotel in Exeter, nineteen rolls of turf, a moose head and a full-sized stuffed bear. Pictures, hairdryers and kettles all figure in the top ten most stolen items.

BLIND SPOT

An attempted raid on a Building Society in East London failed, because the gang's look-out had left his distinctive pebble glasses behind – so that he wouldn't be recognised. As a result, he could hardly see a thing – not even the police closing in.

SHOPLIFTING

A middle-aged woman in a supermarket in Lausanne, Switzerland was caught shoplifting when she fainted from cold, after stuffing a frozen chicken down her bra.

CRIME & MEDIA

A television team making a murder mystery film in an old house near Lubeck in Germany, found the remains of a dead man on the first floor.

Two men who broke out of a Swiss prison announced their escape to a radio station in Lausanne and won a prize for the best listener's news item. The prize of a transistor radio could not be sent to them, because they left no forwarding address.

ASSAULT & ARSON

In 1971 a nineteen year-old seaman in the US Navy was sentenced to six months in the brig, demotion in rank and a $400 fine, for smacking a commanding officer in the face with a chocolate cream pie, as a 'practical joke' to boost his unit's morale. This verdict was passed, despite expert evidence given by tv slapstick comic, Soupy Sales. He told the court that, in his experience of receiving 19,253 pies in the face, this did not amount to assault.

A nineteen year old Australian navy seaman was found guilty of destroying twelve Australian naval aircraft, when he tossed a burning paper aeroplane into a crowded hangar.

In 1976, a twenty-four year-old man in Tulsa, Oklahoma, was convicted of assault and fined twenty dollars, plus thirty-one dollars court costs, for kissing police-woman Perry Burnett's elbow while she attempted to give him a parking ticket.

COUNTERFEITING

The world's only truly international currency, the American dollar, lacks a watermark and metallic strip. Its only protection from forgery is its special blue and red fibre-flecked paper and high-quality indigo printing.

The US Treasury admits it does not know the location of eighty per cent of all the dollar notes which have been printed. The dollar is counterfeited in quantity in Italy, Colombia and the Lebanon. Official statistics claim that Secret Service agents around the world seized $110 million in counterfeit bills in 1988; only ten per cent of these had been passed on to the public.

In 1987 a colour-blind, unemployed US printer was caught red-handed and charged with counterfeiting dollar bills. He had used black ink instead of bright green.

THE HUMAN HOOVER

A Brazilian jewel thief had his little finger surgically modified to enable him to suck up gems through a hole in its tip – by using an intravenous pump and tube, activated when his muscles were flexed. The fifteen millimetre (½ inch) tube ran from the tip of his finger, all the way up to his armpit. The 'human hoover' was arrested by police in Bangkok, in December 1991.

PIRATES

The story-book image of pirates is, in most cases, a long way from the truth.

Some pirates, like Blackbeard, were swashbuckling larger-than-life characters; Blackbeard tied smoking fuses in his hair when he went into battle. Most pirates were just cut-throats and sadists.

No documented accounts of pirates forcing their victims to walk the plank have yet been found. One pirate, named Jack the Baltic did drown his victims the legend may have sprung from this.

The ultimate punishment for a pirate who deserted a battle or stole another pirate's plunder was to be marooned on a desert island, with just a flagon of water, a musket and some ammunition.

Pirates were very democratic. They shared their booty equally and could even vote their captain out of office.

Much new evidence about pirate life has come from Port Royal in Jamaica, one of the great pirate centres of the Caribbean. A earthquake in 1692 caused half the town to slip under the ocean where it remains, preserved a treasure trove of pirate material.

Kuala Lumpur in Malaysia is the epicentre for modern piracy and it is here that the world's first piracy warning centre was opened on 1 October 1992.

In 1992, seventy out of eighty-four reported piratical attacks took place in the Far East. Twenty-one ships were stolen-to-order in the Philippines during this period. Brazil, Venezuela, Ecuador and ports in Nigeria and Angola are all piracy hot spots.

HIDE & SEEK

A former Ministry of Defence police sergeant hid from the police in his wife's tumble-dryer for three years. He had jumped bail after being accused of stealing a car.

A man in Wigan lived for eight years under the floorboards of his council house. He took to his coffin-sized 'tomb' after being suspected by police of a serious crime.

He spent the first two years in total darkness, seeing only his wife, who supplied him with food and drink.

MISTAKEN IDENTITY

A strange case of the mistaken identification of a corpse occurred in Kansas in 1934. The body of a young woman who had been shot to death on a lonely road was positively identified, by forty individuals, as being the body of nineteen different people. The forty 'identifiers' claimed the girl as their wife, daughter, sister or friend. All relatives and friends were later found to be alive.

This is made stranger by the fact that the dead girl was so distinct. She had red hair, unusual scars on both ankles – and she was pregnant.

DETECTION TECHNIQUES

Rotterdam police have pioneered a system of detection using body odours. Police instructor, Jan de Bruin took fifteen years to develop a system for doing this. A custom-built ventilator is used to transfer an odour from the scene of a crime or directly from a suspect's skin, to a chemically-treated cotton swab.

A trained sniffer dog then compares this to over 400 samples stored in an 'odour library', or to a range of cotton swabs containing similar odours.

Researchers at the Metropolitan Police forensic science laboratory in London have developed a computerised method of analyzing shoe-prints.

Not only are our feet distinct in size and shape, but the way we walk also causes certain patterns of wear and tear on our shoes – this can be identified by a-shoe print.

Ear-prints may be another valuable clue to criminal's identity. A US researcher has been collecting ear-prints for more than thirty-eight years and has never found two the same.

Forensic scientists have developed a computerized photography system that can match these and other facial features, recorded by a bank security cameras with video stills shot during a police interview.

The first Photofit system, which offered more than 12 billion permutations of facial characteristics, was officially launched by its inventor, Jacques Penry in 1970.

POLICE COSTS

According to an internal costs-guide released by London's Metropolitan Police, a police dog costs £20.50 a day, a police horse £24.50 a day; a constable gets paid £145 a day and a commander £349 a day. The cost of running a police coach is £2.38 per mile.

ROUGH JUSTICE

Nowhere in the world do judges and lawyers work at such risk as in the Latin American country of Colombia. Some 350 judicial officials have been killed there since 1980 and more than 4,300 judges, one-fifth of the country's total, have been threatened with death.

The threats not only come from the infamous drug cartels but also from 130 guerrilla groups, death squads and paramilitary organisations that operate within the country.

CON AIR

Con Air is the nickname for operations run by the air operations division of the US Marshals' Service.

Since 1984 they have been flying their own aircraft – a fleet of two airliners and five smaller aeroplanes . In 1990 alone, they carried 48,000 inmates – including Colombian drug dealers and serial killers – to thirty-eight American cities.

Each flight carries up to ninety-six hardened criminals. All the passengers travel in leg irons and handcuffs.

PRISONS

About 3,500 people a year are jailed for drunken driving in Sweden, about as many people as are jailed for crimes of violence.

Alcatraz was one of the most notorious prisons in the world. Situated on a fist-shaped island of 90,000 sq metres (22 acres) in San Francisco harbour, it was specially designed to house all the troublemakers in the US prison system.

The first 156 prisoners were brought from Alabama by train (in reinforced railroad cars) and boat. For the first five years – the 'silent years' – they were not allowed to speak.

Fifteen hundred prisoners were kept here during the twenty-nine years the prison – known to its inmates as 'The Rock' – was open. Thirty-nine prisoners tried too escape in fourteen different attempts. Most were recaptured, seven were shot and three drowned. Five remain unaccounted for; their story formed the basis for the Clint Eastwood/Don Siegel movie, *Escape from Alcatraz.*

Al Capone and John Dillinger both served time here but The Rock's most famous prisoner was Robert Stroud, known as the 'Birdman of Alcatraz'. A murderer who spent fifty-three years of his life in jail, Stroud became a bird expert and wrote the definitive *Digest of Bird Diseases* in 1943. He even sold one of his birds to J. Edgar Hoover, head of the FBI. In 1946 he stopped a prison riot during which two guards were killed. He died in November 1963 – still in captivity, but not in Alcatraz.

Alcatraz is now a major tourist attraction with 750,000 visitors a year.

Princetown, one of Britain's bleakest spots, is the highest inhabited town in England. 400 metres (1300 ft) above sea-level, it is home to 2,000 people and the 600 convicts inside Dartmoor Prison, which sits at the town's centre. The whole area is owned by Prince Charles, who is not only Prince of Wales but also Duke of Cornwall. Arthur Conan-Doyle wrote part of *The Hound of the Baskervilles* in the local Duchy Hotel. Prison and town are shrouded by mist or isolated by snow for much of the year.

 Alcatraz was the most secure prison in America. Now the island in San Francisco Bay is a popular tourist resort and visitors can leave if they wish.

PRISONERS

In 1974, a Federal judge in Phoenix, Arizona, dismissed as 'frivolous' a suit filed by a dwarf inmate, who claimed he was being discriminated against in jail.

The prisoner, who was 1.2 m (3 ft 11 in) tall, was serving a sentence for armed robbery. He claimed his civil rights were being violated by the authorities' refusal to redesign his cell to suit his proportions. He claimed his sink and his shower were both out of reach.

Double murderer, Alex Torbet, currently serving a life sentence at Saughton Prison in Edinburgh, has developed an unusual talent. He has become internationally known for his ability to breed an African fish, the tilapia.

The tilapia is important because it is rich in protein and grows quickly and could provide much-needed food in coastal regions of Africa. As a result of Torbet's work, fish farms based on his principles have also been established successfully in Thailand, Indonesia and Bangladesh.

A forty year-old prisoner filed suit in a Federal court asking to be transferred from the Oklahoma Men's State Prison on the grounds that the Bible 'commands man to be fruitful and multiply and replenish the earth.' He said that, because of his enforced sexual segregation, he was unable to carry out his religious stirrings and obey God's word.

TELEPHONES

It is estimated that there are more than 454 million telephones in use in the world, of which 186 million are in Europe, 163 million in North and South America, 88 million in Asia, eight million in Oceania and some seven million in Africa.

Countries which have fewer than ten telephones per 1,000 population include China (7), Pakistan (65), India (5), Indonesia (4) and most of Africa.

The Houston telephone directory is the largest in the world. It runs to 2,889 pages with 939,640 listings.

When Alexander Graham Bell gave the first public demonstration of the telephone at the Centennial World's Fair held in Philadelphia in 1876, the story goes that the Emperor of Brazil picked it up, listened, and exclaimed, 'My God, it talks'. This 'fact' became enshrined in the history books – but it never actually happened. The whole incident was invented by a Brooklyn teacher in 1923 who was trying to make science more interesting for his pupils.

The world's worst wrong number was claimed by a BBC employee in London, who swears that he tried to ring nearby, Walthamstow and got the laundry room of the Empire State Building instead.

The world's longest long-distance police emergency call occurred in 1977 when a woman living at Port Headland in Western Australia was talking on the phone to her brother in Leeds, England. The brother heard strange noises and then the line went dead, so he telephoned his local police who contacted the Port Headland police – after getting the number from international directory inquiries. They sent an officer to the sister's house just eighteen minutes later and found that the woman had been attacked.

Observant viewers might notice that in all American tv cop series, whenever a character gives his telephone number, it begins with area code 555. There is no such code in real life, and this is used by the film-makers to discourage cranks who might try to dial numbers they hear mentioned.

An undertaker in Kansas City in 1889, named Almon Brown Strowger invented the automatic telephone exchange because he suspected that telephone operators were being paid by rival undertakers not to connect customers to him.

There may be no better measure of the links between nations than how often they speak, according to the International Institute of Communications.

The UK spends two billion telephone minutes speaking to other European

Community countries every year and 1.1 billion minutes talking to the US.

Luxembourg makes more international calls than India, which has two thousand times the population.

Japan remains insular. It makes 870 million minutes of outgoing calls, compared with Switzerland's 1.4 billion.

The total volume of international calls was estimated to be 35 billion minutes in 1991; this figure is expected to double by 1995.

On Easter Sunday 1995 nearly every telephone number in Britain will change. The digit 1 will be inserted behind the initial 0 in every dialling code, to provide enough numbers to cope with customer demand due to new technology. The change will cost British Telecom tens of million of pounds and industry £2-300 million.

PHONECARDS

Phonecards originated in Italy in 1976 and are now issued by the phone companies of 150 countries. There are also vast numbers issued for advertising and promotional purposes.

Phonecard collecting has now become a world-wide hobby. In Germany alone, there are an estimated 40,000 collectors with their own magazines, clubs, catalogues and exchange fairs.

Some cards are very valuable; the highest price ever paid for one in Europe was £4,000.

Japan has one million collectors. The first Japanese card ever issued last sold at auction for £28,000, making it the Penny Black of the electronic age.

Other rarities include the only phone card issued by East Germany, and so-called Closed User Group cards, used by people who work on oil rigs, on military bases or in prison.

 A phonecard collector – or should they be called phoneatilists – displays his hard-won prizes. Queueing up outside phoneboxes in the rain for spent cards is just one of the hazards of the profession.

CODE TALKERS

During World War II, several hundred Navajo Indians, serving in the Marines, were used to transmit and receive radio messages in the Navajo language. Needless to say, the Japanese found this 'code' unbreakable.

STEVE & NEVETS

Steven Woodmore is the world's fastest talker. He can speak up to 638 words per minute if he's rehearsed the passage beforehand. That is 10.25 words a second, four times faster than most people talk, three times faster than most people read and twice as fast as most people think. Woodmore is a salesman for a branch of Curries, the electrical shop.

Steven Briers is the world's fastest backwards talker. Steve, or 'Nevets' as he prefers to be known, reverses the letters in each word of a sentence but keeps the order of the words in the sentence the same. He first discovered he had this talent when he was a kid. He can read the lyrics of the Queen album. *Night At The Opera,* a total of 2,343 words, backwards in nine minutes, 58.44 seconds. Briers works as a disc jockey and runs a mobile Karaoke show, singing the words backwards as they come up on the screen.

TWIN SPEECH

Identical twins, Virginia and Grace Kennedy from California, started speaking in their own private language – despite the fact that they understand English, German and sign language.

It all began when they were seventeen months old. Their mother recalls that one of them would hold up an object, suggest a name for it, and the other would agree. In their new language, Virginia called herself, *Cabenga* and Grace called herself, *Poto*.

Scientists call this phenomenon *idioglossia* or 'twin speech'. If they manage to unravel the twin's private language, they may be able to decipher the scientific riddle of whether children are born with a genetically determined brain mechanism for developing language, or whether language is acquired through exposure to the written word.

SHORTHAND

Shorthand is supposed to have been invented in Rome in 63 BC, by a certain, Marco Tiro. His system contained about three thousand symbols and was so popular that it remained in use for six hundred years. Marco Tiro's shorthand was revived by fifteenth-century scholars and is thought to have been used to record Martin Luther's speeches. One of the symbols of the Tiro method is still in use throughout the western world – the ampersand (&) sign.

Modern shorthand systems like Pitmans, which uses twenty-six strokes for consonants, plus a number of dashes and dots for vowels, make it possible to write as fast as it is possible to understand human speech, (roughly 230 words per minute). Most of us speak at about 100 words a minute, using about 1,500 clauses per hour.

WORDS & PHRASES

All the following words are derived from Arabic:

❂ *Algebra* comes from *aljebr*, meaning a reunion of broken parts.

❂ *Average* comes from *awairy,* the term for damaged goods. Original usage referred to the amount of ship's cargo that could be expected to be lost through unavoidable accidents.

❂ *Tabby*, as in 'tabby cat' comes from *attabi*, a cloth with stripes in various colours, first manufactured in an area of Baghdad.

A Seattle man has created a new word – *catmatic*. The opposite of dogmatic, it means one who pussy-foots around.

Sarcophagus derives from the Greek for 'flesh eater', so-called because of the corrosive effect of early limestone coffins on the bodies interred inside them.

The mulberry bush of the nursery rhyme was really a tree in the yard of Wakefield Prison. Prisoners used to walk round it for hours, so the expression 'Here we go round the mulberry bush' came to mean getting nowhere, or an exercise in futility.

To highlight inconsistencies of pronunciation, George Bernard Shaw invented a new way of spelling 'fish', namely, 'Ghoti'. That is 'gh' as in enough, 'o' as in women and 'ti' as in nation.

QWERTYUIOP

The layout of the letters on computer keyboards dates back to the birth of the typewriter in the 1870s. The first such machines couldn't keep up with quick-fingered typists and as a result the keys kept on getting tangled up. The inventors couldn't find a way of mechanically solving this problem, so they had to slow the typist down, by designing the most inconvenient and confusing arrangement of typewriter keys possible. The so-called QWERTY keyboard (named after the first six letters on its top row), has survived as standard.

FIRST FAX

You may think that the fax is a recent invention but the first faxes were sent more than a hundred years ago.

There are various claims as to who got there first. Alexander Bain is recorded as having taken out a patent on a fax machine in 1843. A certain F.C.

Bakewell described his own, 'copying telegraph' in his book *Electric Science,* published in 1853.

Neither of these may have actually been built but the 'pentélégraphe' invented by an Italian physics professor named, Giovanni Caselli certainly was. It began operating between Paris and Lyon in 1866 and transmitted nearly five thousand faxes in the first year.

Made of cast iron and standing more than two metres (6 ½ ft) high, this primitive but effective fax worked as follows. The sender wrote a message on a sheet of tin in non-conducting ink. The sheet was then fixed to a curved metal plate and scanned by a needle, three lines to the millimetre.

The signals were carried by telegraph to the receiving fax machine, on which the needle marked out the message in Prussian blue ink, the colour produced by a chemical reaction as the paper was soaked in potassium ferro-cyanide.

To ensure that both needles scanned at exactly the same rate, two extremely accurate clocks were used to trigger a pendulum which, in turn was linked to gears and pulleys that controlled the needles.

TELEGRAMS

When General Sir Charles Napier captured the province of Sind, on 17 February 1843, he sent a one-word telegram from India to the Foreign Office. It simply said *Peccavi*, a Latin word meaning 'I have sinned.'

MORSE CODE

The first message that Samuel F.B. Morse tapped out on the world's first telegraph link – from the Capitol Building in Washington DC to Baltimore – in May, 1844, was 'What hath God wrought!'.

Morse code was actually devised by Morse's associate Alfred L. Vail.

BAR CODES

Bar codes and the magnetic strip on the back of credit cards are the most visible signs of the new fast-growing industry in 'automatic identification techniques' (auto ID for short).

Essentially, auto ID can be defined as the entry of data into computers without using keystrokes. It includes radio frequency tags – used in the identification of animals, vehicles and even prisoners – voice recognition and machine vision systems. Futuristic auto-ID techniques include identification systems that check the pattern of blood vessels on the human retina, a characteristic which is as unique to an individual as a fingerprint.

The patent on many aspects of the bar code is owned by a company called, Symbol, who license it out to other companies.

In 1991, Symbol released a new, two-dimensional, patterned bar code, capable of storing large quantities of information. The entire Gettysburg Address – about 250 words – can be carried on a bar code measuring just 57 mm x 64 mm (2¼ x 2½ in).

COMPUTERS

The world's first computer museum opened in Boston in 1985. Among its exhibits is the Whirlwind computer, built with vacuum tubes in the 1950s at the Massachusetts Institute of Technology (MIT). The Whirlwind was rescued from the scrap-heap by the presidents of two major computer companies who, in their youth, had worked on the machine. It took five years to build and filled a whole building. The computer was 'interviewed' on tv in 1952 by the famous US newscaster, Ed Murrow. On air, it worked out how much the American Indians would have received, in interest, if they had invested the twenty-four dollars they got for Manhattan at six per cent per annum.

The largest computer ever built, the 175 tonne SAGE, ran the US Air Force defence system from 1958 to 1983 – displaying on huge screens, every aircraft movement in US airspace.

Thomas Watson, chairman of IBM predicted in 1943: 'There is a world market for about five computers'.

ENIAC (the Electronic Numerical Integrator and Computer) was twenty-four metres (80 ft) long, 2.4 m (8 ft) high, weighed 30 tonnes and had 18,000 vacuum tubes and 70,000 resistors. Unveiled in February 1946, it calculated the trajectory of shells for the US Army at a speed one hundred times slower than a modern personal computer.

ENIAC was fitted with 4,000 red neon tubes which lit up to show the functions of various parts of the machine so that faults could be traced. Ever since, science fiction machines have been depicted as having flashing lights all over them.

Five years after unveiling ENIAC, its inventors, Dr J. Presper Eckert and his partner developed 'Univac 1', the first commercial computer.

EARLY LEARNING

At least 45,000 titles survive of books, published before January, 1501. If we assume that an average edition comprised 500 copies, that makes a total of twenty million books in circulation at a time when there were only a few hundred thousand readers in each generation.

PENCILS

The pencil's origins lie in Ancient Roman society and two drawing implements; a *pencillus* or little tail – a tiny brush used to paint fine outlines – and the *plumbum*, a small lead disc (also used by the Egyptians and Greeks) for ruling lines on papyrus, to keep lettering even.

By the fourteenth century, artists were using a kind of 'pencil' with rods of lead, zinc and silver, held in a wooden case. This 'pencil' was first described in 1565 by Conrad Gesner of Zurich as a footnote in his *Treatise on Fossils*.

The previous year, an extraordinary discovery had been made in the Borrowdale mines in Cumbria. It was a deposit of graphite (pure black carbon), in a form solid enough to be sawn into sheets and made into pencil leads.

Called at the time, *plumbago* (that which acts (writes) like lead), this was the only such deposit found and was of immense value. It was only mined six weeks a year and the graphite was then taken to London in wagons, escorted by armed guards. Exports of the ore were prohibited.

Cumberland graphite, which we now know owes its unique origin to volcanic activity, has remained the only known deposit which can be used in its natural state, but graphite hasn't been mined in Cumberland for more than eighty years.

For many years, the English Guild of Pencil Makers hand-carved the wooden cases for the leads and held a world monopoly on the finished product.

The first chemical analysis of plumbago, by K.W. Scheele, was carried out in 1779. The material proved to be a form of carbon. In 1789, it was named *graphite*, from the Greek word meaning, 'to write'.

The modern pencil industry imports pure graphite in lumps from Mexico, Korea, Sri Lanka and the Malagasy Republic.

The graphite is reduced to a powder, purified and then mixed with various binding materials. The mass, in the form of slurry, is ground to a particle size of below one-thousandth of an inch. The degree of hardness and softness of a pencil depends on the proportions of clay added to the pure graphite. The more clay, the harder the pencil.

After this grinding process, all moisture is extracted and the graphite-mass is subjected to extremely high pressure. It is hammered into cylinders, extruded into strips, cut into lengths, heated to over 1,200 °C (2,200 °F) and then impregnated with various oils and waxes, ready for use.

The best wood for pencil-making is incense cedar.

LIVING MASTERPIECES

Every year since 1933 at the Laguna Festival of Arts in California, local people have staged their Pageant of the Masters, in which they recreate works of art, using live models.

This is a highly- sophisticated and technical version of a centuries-old tradition of *tableaux vivants* (living pictures). The models remain absolutely motionless and the three-dimensional 'cast' is made to look two-dimensional with special lighting, make-up and sets.

These 'living picture' pageants were well-established all over Europe as far back as a thousand years ago. Mounted on 'floats', they were initially staged in public squares, to illustrate biblical scenes to people who couldn't read. The range of topics gradually broadened from religion to mythology, history, art, literature and politics.

The arrival of an important visitor was always marked by such a pageant. Elaborate versions were staged on river-barges, or in harbours in cities like Florence, Amsterdam, Bristol and Antwerp.

When Charles Dickens visited the United States in 1842, he witnessed a presentation at a New York theatre in his honour, in which 'frozen' recreations of scenes from some of his novels were staged.

The Pageant of The Masters at Laguna is a two-hour evening presentation staged in a beautiful outdoor amphitheatre. More than one hundred people of all ages take part, bringing to life sculptures, tapestries and famous paintings, like Leonardo da Vinci's *Last Supper* . Such careful attention to detail creates a powerful illusion.

UNUSUAL ARTISTS

Morris Katz is both the world's most prolific artist and the fastest.

He has sold more than 200,000 paintings, outdoing even Pablo Picasso. He has had his own cable tv show and cabaret act and is the author of *Paint Good and Fast*, which documents his technique, which he calls 'instant art.'

His fastest painting was a 30 x 40 cm (12 in x 16 in) canvas of a child in the snow, which he painted in thirty seconds with an additional eight seconds to frame it.

A Polish Jew, born in 1932 in a small rural village, he was sent to Nazi concentration camp at the age of nine, but managed to survive. He first began painting at the age of thirteen, while living in a displaced persons camp in Germany. His mother paid for his first art lessons with handfuls of chocolates, a rare commodity at the time; Katz would later repay this debt by creating a series of edible portraits out of chocolate.

He emigrated with his mother to New York in 1959 and began a long period of rigorous study in classical painting techniques and colour experimentation. This led to his development of 'instant art' – a technique that relies on the fast, deft use of the palette knife to mix and apply colour, with the use of toilet tissue as a brush.

His portrait of Pope Paul VI has sold over three million copies.

Devonshire artist, Bob Bradshaw specialises in painting miniature watercolours

 The pioneering French artist Aquabouse demonstrates his dung painting technique by producing a portrait of the animal it came from.

of local landscapes. His paintings, which measure around 25 sq mm (1 in sq) are often used to adorn doll's houses.

Rob Perry from Britain's Black Country has an unusual speciality. He only paints at night.

Jet Art was the brainchild of German-born, Juergen Prince von Anhalt who creates canvases by hurling paint into the exhaust of jet engines. He claims that the idea came to him a hotel room in Jerusalem during a fit of despondency after his plans for a Middle East Peace Chain (composed of 50,000 people holding hands from Cairo to Jerusalem), had to be abandoned at the last minute. He planned to establish a Jet Art studio, containing seven Jumbo Jet engines.

UNDERWATER ART

France's first underwater museum of modern art has been established ten metres (30 ft) under the surface of the Mediterranean, off the coast of Antibes. Its founder is Régis Blanchet and the museum consists of seven small statues of samurai warriors made of concrete.

Jamy Verheylewegen is the world's first underwater painter. He has produced more than 350 paintings since 1983, at depths of up to thirty-seven metres (120 ft), using oil paints on a synthetic fabric, mounted on an easel weighted-down with six kilos of lead.

Belgian scuba diver, Verheylewegen took up this usual craft after crushing a nerve in his back, which crippled him for eighteen months. His paintings are often exhibited underwater and are hung 'up' with lead weights fastened to their lower corners. Those who wish to view them are taken down by bathyscaphe, dressed in frogmen's outfits.

RECORDS

The first sound-effects LP ever to get into the UK Top 100 was produced by the BBC Radiophonic Workshop. Called Death and Horror, it featured such tracks as, 'Head Chopped Off' and 'Red Hot Poker in the Eye'. According to a spokesman, all were produced by 'mistreating large white cabbages'.

The longest word ever featured on a single may be; *Taumatawhakatang-ihanakoauquotamateaturipukakpikimauncahoronukupokaiwhenuakitanatahu*. It features in The *Lone Ranger* by Quantum Jump, issued in 1977.

The smallest single ever made was a recording of *God Save The King*, produced by HMV in 1924. It measured just 35 mm (1⅜ in) in diameter.

Humpin' was the title of the first LP by an Arab/Israeli band called Abu Hafla, meaning ' enjoyable gathering.' The band consists of a ten-piece classical Arab orchestra, three Israeli singers, a Moroccan drummer, an Egyptian tambourinist and a blind Iraqi bongo player.

Kinky Friedman and the Texas Jewboys recorded a song entitled *There Ain't No Instant Replay in the Football Game of Life*. Bobby Bare recorded the song, *Drop-Kick Me, Jesus, Through the Goal Posts of Life*.

The first release from Gammill Records in Denver, issued in 1985, was a musical interpretation of the IBM share-price movements. It was called *Rhapsody in Big Blue*.

    The tune is based on daily differences in the share-price transposed into shifts up and down the C-major scale. When the volume of traded shares increases, so does the volume of the music. The buying or selling of shares by IBM employees themselves is recorded as high or low chimes.

MUSIC

The Bach family produced sixty-two professional musicians, including Johann Sebastian, between 1600 and 1800.

The quietest piece of music ever recorded was John Cage's, *4' 33"* , a piano piece composed in 1952. The composer instructs the pianist to walk on stage, sit down, wait in silence for four minutes and thirty-three seconds and then walk off stage again.

The term 'heavy metal' in music derives from a phrase written by the American author, William Burroughs. It was first used in a track called, *Born To Be Wild* by the band Steppenwolf in 1968.

On average, Mozart wrote a new piece of music every twelve days during his short but busy life.

Jamey Turner is one of only three professional glass players in the world. His instrument consists of sixty fine brandy glasses of different sizes, which are fixed by rubber bands to a special table. The glasses are tuned to different notes by removing or adding distilled water. He produces notes or chords by wetting his fingers and running them round the rims of the glasses.

Musical glasses have a 300 year-old history. Mozart gave his first glass-playing concert at the age of seventeen; other famous players include, Marie Antoinette and Benjamin Franklin. Scores for the instrument have been written by Haydn and John Philip Sousa.

Ian Watson, the artistic director of a marathon Vivaldi concert, held at London's Royal Festival Hall in September 1992 was fed glucose through an intravenous drip to enable him to work fourteen hours without a break.

FACT This gives a whole new meaning to playing with a bicycle. Is he trying to play "Ticket to Ride" or "My White Bicycle"?

FACT In 1903, the biggest real estate sign ever built was erected on California's Mount Cook – HOLLYWOODLAND. The estate survives to this day as a small suburb to the film capital of the world.

More than half of all British government spending on music – sixty-two million pounds in 1987-88 – was spent on military bands.

The earliest recorded use of the word 'jazz' is in *Uncle Josh in Society*, a 1909 Columbia recording by Cal Stewart.

The phrase 'honky-tonk' first appeared in the 24 February 1894-issue of *The Daily Ardmoreite,* published in Ardmore, Oklahoma. The report reads that 'the honk-a-tonk last night was well-attended by ball-heads, bachelors and leading citizens.

Rock and roll were both used as verbs in the Middle Ages in England. Shakespeare wrote in *Venus and Adonis*: 'My throbbing heart shall rock thee day and night.' A nineteenth century sea shanty contained the line: 'Oh do, me Johnny Bowker, come rock 'n' roll me over.'

Charles Dickens, in *The Posthumous Papers of the Pickwick Club,* first published in 1837, uses the word 'funky'.

Charles Conrad took a Jerry Lee Lewis cassette with him to the moon, onboard *Apollo XI*.

The first fade-out effect on a record occurs on *The New Call of the Freaks* by jazz pianist, Luis Russell, which ends with a ghostly, drunken chant of 'Stick out your can, here comes the garbage man.'

SONG WRITERS

Actor, John Howard Payne, who wrote *Home Sweet Home*, was an American expatriate. When he died, his body was exhumed from its grave in North Africa and brought back to Washington for reburial.

George Cory, who wrote the lyrics for *I Left My Heart in San Francisco*, died there in 1978. Cory wrote the song with tunesmith, Douglas Cross during a bout of home sickness while in New York in 1946. It lay unrecorded for fifteen years, until Tony Bennett used it in his act at the city's Fairmont Hotel in 1961. The song was adopted as the city's official anthem eight years later.

The famous song, *Amazing Grace* was written by a British slave trader-turned Church of England minister named John Newton (1725-1807).

THE ELVIS ESTATE

The eighty-two page inventory of Elvis Presley's estate, after his death in August 1977, included a complete inventory of his mansion Graceland.

The house was filled with statues of tigers, lions, elephants, dogs, birds, a ram, a whale, an eagle and a dolphin. Elvis collected statuettes of Joan of Arc and Venus de Milo; one of the latter came complete with an electric waterfall.

For transport, he had two Stutz Blackhawks, a Ferrari, a Cadillac, an International Harvester Scout, a Jeep, a Ford Bronco, a custom-built Chevy pickup, three tractors, seven motorcycles, seven golf carts, three mobile homes and six horses.

He had eighteen tv sets, including the seventeen-inch colour set installed in the ceiling above his 2.7 metre (9ft) square bed. His wardrobe consisted of one hundred pairs of trousers, twenty-one capes, three cartons of shoes and three jewel-studded vests.

His trophy room was decorated with his army discharge papers, forty-

 Elvis Presley's last home, Graceland, is one of the most popular tourist haunts in America. The Elvis Presley Estate licenses thousands of products every year.

one plaques, thirty-two photo albums of his films, thirty script albums, plus scrapbooks and trophies from his fans, record companies and karate clubs.

BUDDY'S GLASSES

Buddy Holly's glasses were found twenty years after his death, in court archives near the site where his plane crashed at Clear lake, Iowa, on 3 February 1959. The glasses did not have any lenses in them.

The local sheriff who found them along, with a watch belonging to the other passenger, J.P. 'Big Bopper' Richardson, told reporters: 'This stuff wasn't with the other personal effects and wasn't listed in our records. My guess is that it was found later and turned in.'

TELEVISION

In June 1992, a Japanese electronics company unveiled their new product – a tv with a one-metre (40 inch) screen only 76 mm (3 in) thick.

Sesame Street was such a huge hit in Pago Pago, the government considered naming the island's main street after it.

In a 1970's a survey conducted among American children aged four to six, asked the question: 'Which do you like better, tv or Daddy?' Forty-four percent of them said they preferred tv.

I Love Lucy, first screened on 15 October 1951, was tv's first genuine hit and the first tv series filmed with a three-camera set-up before a live studio audience, now standard practice for sitcoms. Its pulling power was such that, on the occasion of the screening of Eisenhower's inauguration, only twenty-seven million people watched the President's swearing-in, while forty-four million watched Lucy have her baby on the other channel.

The first full-length feature film shown on American tv was *The Heart of New York*, the story of the inventors of the washing machine.

The first commercial aired on US television was in 1941, for Bulova watches. The advert cost the company nine dollars.

The first tv commercial shown in Britain was an advert for the *Daily Mail*, shown at a demonstration by John Logie Baird at the National Radio Exhibition in Olympia on 26 September 1928. It was screened on a dozen sets and viewed by an audience of fifty.

The big hit tv series of the early 1990s in Russia was *The Rich Also Cry*, a soap opera donated to the country as 'humanitarian aid' by Mexico. All the voices, male and female, were dubbed by just one man.

TV ACCIDENTS

A 1992 UK Government report, produced by the Home Accident Surveillance System (HASS) of the Department of Trade and Industry, revealed that every year, 7,000 television viewers end up in hospital – the victims of tv-related accidents.

Accidents reported include the following:

✪ Watching a football match on the tv – Rovers scored and patient accidentally hit wall with hand.

✪ Watching tv – patient pushed polo mint down ear.

✪ While watching boxing – patient punched television.

✪ Dancing to music on television – patient dislocated knee.

✪ Watching rugby on tv – Ireland scored, patient jumped and banged hand on chandelier.

✪ Playing Peek-A-Boo in lounge curtains – patient tripped and hit head on tv legs.

✪ Watching tv – patient bitten by dog for no reason.

✪ Copying tv program, doing push squats – patient fell on face on carpet.

✪ Watching tv – patient got excited. So did dog. Dog bit patient's hand.

✪ Taking in washing – patient heard goal scored on tv, ran, caught foot and fell.

✪ Eating dinner while watching tv – patient accidentally struck eye with fork.

✪ Going to switch television over – patient fell over dog.

✪ Patient poked his own finger into his eye – whilst watching tv.

✪ Watching tv. Saw man covered in blood – patient fainted and hit head.

✪ Eating biscuits while watching tv – patient got piece of biscuit stuck in throat.

✪ Watching tv with son. Son pointed to tv – poked patient in the eye.

✪ Eating tea while watching tv – patient put nutshell up nose.

THE LONE RANGER

The Lone Ranger, also known as John Reid, was first developed as a character by George W. Trendle – then working at radio station WXYZ in Detroit – with writer Fran Striker. the program was first aired on 30 January 1933, and continued for 2,956 episodes over the next twenty years.

Among those who played the title character in that time were, George Seaton (the first), Jack Deeds (only lasted two days), Earle Graser (who invented the call, 'Hi yo Silver') and Brace Breemer. The Lone Ranger most familiar to modern tv audiences was Clayton Moore.

Tonto was played by Jay Silverheels, who died on 5 March 1980 of pneumonia, aged sixty-seven. A Mohawk Indian, he was born in Canada and named Harold J. Smith; he legally changed his name in 1971.

He went to the US in 1949 as a member of the Canadian national lacrosse team and broke into films playing an Indian prince in *The Captain from Castille* (1947). He subsequently appeared in many movies including *Key Largo* with Humphrey Bogart and Lauren Bacall, and John Wayne's Oscar-winning film, *True Grit*. In 1979, he became the first North American Indian to be awarded a star on Hollywood Boulevard.

Silver, the Lone Ranger's faithful horse, died in 1977, aged twenty-nine.

TARZAN

In the first Tarzan movie, *Tarzan of the Apes*, starring Elmo Lincoln, all the monkeys were played by football players from the New Orleans Athletic Club, dressed in ape suits.

The lion in the film was real, however. Despite having been sedated, in one scene the lion attacked Lincoln, who later recalled: 'When the lion jumped me, I stabbed him and he died. After a stunned moment, we continued shooting and I stepped down on him, the remaining air in his lungs escaping with a loud whoosh. I was already shaken and you should have seen me jump.'

Lincoln had borrowed the knife from a local woman who rushed off after the incident saying: 'Wait until I tell Bill tonight that I cut up the pig with a knife that had just killed a lion.'

James H. Pierce, the fourth of fifteen Tarzans and the last of the silent era, was the only Tarzan to be discovered by the character's creator, Edgar Rice Burroughs. The two-metre (6 ft 4 in)-tall Pierce played the ape man in a 1927 release, *Tarzan and the Golden Lion*, which also featured Boris Karloff (later to be immortalised on screen as Frankenstein) in his screen debut, as a tribal chieftain.

DISNEY CARTOONS

For the first eighteen years of his life, the voice of Mickey Mouse was provided by Walt Disney himself. For the next forty years, it was provided by James MacDonald, who was also head of the sound effects department at Disney's Burbank Studios. Among the problems he had to solve was how to produce the sound of a shimmering spider's web.

For more than sixty years, Donald Duck's voice was provided by Clarence Nash, who died on 20 February 1985. He also did the voices for Huey, Dewie and Louie, for Donald's girlfriend, Daisy, for Jiminy Cricket and for some of the dogs in *101 Dalmatians*.

Disney was an obsessive perfectionist. He ordered the entire cartoon of *Snow White* to be re drawn five times.

Pinocchio artist, Vladimir Tytla shot miles of cine film in the Italian quarter of Los Angeles as research for the drawings of Stromboli the puppet-maker.

Other artists sat for hours in the viewing room of a swimming pool, studying the shimmer of underwater light for the shipwreck scene.

For *Bambi*, Disney sent two cameramen on a seven-month safari through the rugged area around Mt Katahdin in the state of Maine, on the east coast of the United States, to film all aspects of nature, as reference material for his team of city-bred artists.

Snow White, the world's first animated full-length feature in colour, took 750 artists and inkers three years and two million drawings to complete. Only one-eighth of these were used in the final eighty-three-minute film.

Snow White's body movements were based on a young dancer named Margie Belcher.

In 1959, Disneyland was closed down for the day to allow Nikita Kruschev, the then Soviet premier, to visit. The only other visitors present were security men and carefully screened celebrities. Kruschev had threatened to end peace talks with the American government unless he got his outing.

DISNEYLAND

In the first twenty-six years that Disneyland in California was open, there were six accidental deaths. The first murder there was in March 1981, when an eighteen year-old was stabbed to death after an argument at Tomorrow Land.

FILMS

The Chinese call film, 'electric shadows'. Extras in Hollywood are called, 'atmosphere people'

The Rank Odeon at Salisbury in Wiltshire has the only fifteenth-century cinema foyer in the world. The cinema was built on the site of the ancient house of a local wool merchant, which had a preservation order on it. So now patrons pass through a carefully-preserved hall, complete with minstrels' gallery, carved oak screen and timbered roof to get to the auditorium.

William Castle was a film director who established a reputation as the 'King of Gimmicks'. He once offered viewers of his movie, *Macabre* life insurance in case they died of fright. The total insurance was provided by Lloyds of London at a cost of $5,000. A special preview of the film was arranged in a disused cemetery. The movie was screened on a tomb.

For his movie, *Homicidal,* audiences were offered a refund if they left during the 'fright break' ten minutes before the end. No wonder Castle's autobiography was called, *Step Right Up! I'm Gonna Scare the Pants Off America.*

Robert L. Lippert, a Hollywood producer, once shot five Westerns concurrently using the same locations, cast and sets. Lippert saved money by filming all the chases, saloon scenes and brawls simultaneously. He completed each movie at a cost of $50,000.

Hollywood's last major working movie ranch – Big Sky Movie Ranch, the place where *Rawhide, Gunsmoke* and many other classics were shot, was auctioned off in one of the largest land sales ever held in the western United States on 13 June 1987.

Arthur L. Mayer, an auditor and publicist for Sam Goldfish – later Sam Goldwyn of MGM fame – once trained seventy parrots to squawk the name of Mae West's new picture, *It Ain't No Sin*. When he discovered that the title had been changed to *I'm No Angel*, he left Hollywood for New York.

Mel Blanc, the man who provided the voice of Bugs Bunny was allergic to carrots.

HOLLYWOOD SIGN

The world-famous landmark on Mount Lee originally read, HOLLYWOODLAND. It was designed to advertise a real-estate development in 1932, a deal which involved Mack Sennett, the early movie tycoon famous for his Keystone comedies. Despondent actress, Peg Entwhistle leapt to her death off the 'H' in 1932. The original sign was illuminated by 4,000 light bulbs.

In 1978 – Hollywood's seventy-fifth anniversary – a campaign was started by Alice Cooper and Gene Autry to raise money to build a new sign, as the old one was in a dilapidated condition. A glistening new HOLLYWOOD sign, four stories high and 120 metres (400 ft) long, is now in place. It costs $27,700 at the time.

Hank Berger, a disco marketing consultant, acquired the rights to the remains of the old sign, and sold off numbered plaques, each containing a 33 mm (1⁵⁄₁₆ in) square of the original metal, mounted with a hand-tinted photo of the sign in its heyday and an appreciation written by Berger himself.

OSCARS

An Oscar weighs 3.6 kg (8 lb) is 33 cm (13 in) high and is made of 92.5 per cent tin and 7.5 per cent copper with a twenty-four carat gold finish.

There are many stories as to how it got its name but the generally accepted one is that when she saw the statue, the then librarian of the Academy, Margaret Herrick, said it reminded her of her Uncle Oscar.

The trophies are manufactured by the Dodge Trophy Company in Carson California, about eighty miles south of Los Angeles, at a cost of $190 a time.

The first Academy Awards ceremony, held in 1927, was attended by just 250 people; the ceremony now has a world-wide audience of more than a quarter of a billion. At that first ceremony it took just five minutes to distribute the awards; in 1984 it took a record three hours and forty minutes.

4,244 members of the Academy of Motion Picture Arts and Sciences vote in the secret ballot for the Oscars.

RADIO

The first advertisement on Radio Luxembourg in the early 1930s was for Bile Beans, a laxative.

The world's longest-running radio serial was the Australian, Blue Hill, which ran for twenty-seven years and 5,795 episodes before ending on 30 September 1976. The sole scriptwriter for all this time was Gwen Meredith, in real life, Mrs Ainsworth Harrison MBE.

THEATRE

When the stage manager of the Brewhouse Theatre in Taunton, Somerset uttered the traditional cry 'Is there a doctor in the house?' after an elderly woman had fallen down the steps during a fire alert, fifty-seven people in the audience stood up. They were all from a nearby hospital.

One of the most unusual entertainers ever to appear on the stage was Joseph Pujol, better known by his stage name Le Pétomane. His talent was to play an unusual wind instrument. Put it another way: he was an amazing farter.

Pujol could imitate instruments, produce machine-gun farts, cannon-roar farts and a wide repertoire of other sounds. For twenty years he toured all over Europe, always dressed in a red coat and black satin knickerbockers. Pujol lived to be eighty-eight.

Romeo and Juliet was staged in the Tibetan language for the first time in August 1981. Romeo was played by a former miner.

Pablo Picasso wrote a play called Desire Caught By The Tail, which, when it was first performed, starred Jean-Paul Satre and Simone de Beauvoir and was such a miserable failure that it has rarely been staged since. Its main characters are Fat Anxiety, Thin Anguish and Big Foot.

FESTIVALS

The world's first festival for grandmothers was staged in July 1992 in Bodo in Norway. Grannies were invited to skydive, ride motorcycles, race horses and scuba dive in the frigid waters of the North Sea, fifty miles above the Arctic Circle. At the event a seventy nine year-old great grandmother named, Elida Andersen became the world's oldest bungy-jumper.

The big annual event in the Spanish town of Buñol is La Tomatina, a mass fight with 68,000 kg (150,000 lb) of ripe tomatoes. The event has its origins in 1944, when the local fair was disrupted by troublemakers who threw tomatoes at the procession. Now the fair has become the side-show to the tomato fight, which lasts for an hour and a half, before all the participants – red from head to toe – are hosed down.

This is one of more than 3,000 fiestas staged in Spain every year. At Castrillo, an athletic man is chosen as the *calocho* – the naughty devil – and is made to leap over new-born babies laid on mattresses in the street, to exorcise the threat of hernia disease.

FIRE-EATING

The inflammatory art of fire-eating has had many practitioners, including Ivan Ivanitz Chabert, billed in 1818 as 'The Only Really Incombustible Man.'

He could: drink boiling oil and wash his hands in it; forge a bar of hot iron with his feet and dance on it; put burning wax on his tongue and allow a seal to be taken of it; eat burning charcoal; inhale the flame of a torch; bathe his feet in molten lead; pour *aqua fortis* on steel filings and then trample them with his bare feet; and rub a bare shovel on his arms and legs.

FACT Here is a man that no policeman would dare to breathalyse. The ancient art of fire-eating continues to astonish, not least because no one can figure out why anyone would want to do it in the first place.

FANTASTIC SPORTS!

HOLES-IN-ONE

The youngest golfer ever to hole a ball in one was Coby Orr of Colorado at the fifth hole ninety-four metres (103 yd) on a course at San Antonio, Texas, in 1975. He was five years old at the time.

According to 'Golf Digest', the chances of hitting a hole-in-one from the tee are 33,616 to 1, yet a Californian author called Scott Palmer has done it eighteen times since June 1983. Four of his holes-in-one came on consecutive days in October and the average length of all eighteen was 209 yards (190 m). He has also hit the pin fifty other times. All these shots were achieved with the same ball – a seemingly indestructible Spalding Top Flite XL No 2.

Two unusual holes-in-one recorded by J. Eckert Goodman Jr in *Sports Illustrated* and *The American Golfer* are:

✪ James Cash Jr's experience on 18 November, 1929, on the sixteenth hole of the Belmont Springs Country Club in Massachusetts. His ball landed on the rim of the cup, but was helped in by an earth tremor.

✪ Jack Ackerman was playing at the Bay of Quinte Club of Belleville, Ontario, in 1934. His ball was also resting on the lip of the cup when a butterfly struck it with enough force to knock it in.

Seventy-four year old Margaret Weldon scored two holes-in-one on consecutive days on the seventh hole at a golf course in Florida, coached by her husband. Margaret is totally blind.

In Japan it is advisable to insure against getting a hole-in-one as you are then obliged to buy your partner's dinner, be generous to your caddies and take home souvenirs for your friends – all of which can cost more than £1500.

More than twenty leading Japanese insurance companies offer hole-in-one cover. The odds of achieving it on a round of eighteen holes were estimated by one company as being 0.0002993 per cent.

STREET FOOTBALL

Street football, a historic ritual of semi-organised violence, is still played in a dozen places in Britain – the most famous being Ashbourne in Derbyshire – during the period around Shrove Tuesday (Pancake Day).

In these games there may be as many as four hundred players from neighbouring villages with the goals being separated by up to three or four miles of open countryside.

The first recorded game was at Sedgefield, County Durham in 1027. Edward II tried to ban it from London in 1314; in 1349, Edward III tried to ban it altogether, claiming it interfered with archery practice.

Each game has particular variations on a basic theme: a ball is thrown up somewhere near the centre between the two villages and a desperate scrum begins, with the aim of carrying, pushing and shoving the ball to the opposing village. 'Runners' break out with the ball and gain as much ground as they can before being buried under a sea of bodies.

Street football of a more complex but equally violent kind has been played once a year on the streets of Florence for hundreds of years. Historians believe this event, the *Calcio*, may stem from the kind of football played by the Roman Legions – part training exercise, part gladiatorial combat – and that they had learnt it from the Greeks.

There are four teams – White, Blue, Red and Green, named after the four leading quarters of the city – each with twenty-seven players and a standard-bearer. Everyone is in Medieval costume.

A total of 530 participants are involved in staging this elaborate event. Everything is overseen by the Major General Sergeant, who rides around in armour on a white charger. He commands numerous others including Halberdiers, Sergeants of the Eight of Watch and Word, Bombardiers, Drummers, Captains of the Riding Bands and many more, drawn from the city's entire social structure.

The opposing teams use any possible trick or method to get the ball into the opponents' net and games can be extremely violent. The net contains four keepers and a tent. Ends are changed after every point. The prize they are all fighting for is a white heifer.

SOCCER

One of the strangest soccer matches ever played in Britain was one between two teams who had varying handicaps: one lot had their arms tied to their sides and were bootless; the others tottered on two-metre (6 ft) high stilts.

HOME & AWAY

A coach load of Celtic supporters travelled one thousand miles from Glasgow in Scotland to Nuremburg in Germany to watch their team play, only to discover they had come to the wrong venue. Once inside the stadium they found themselves isolated in a silent crowd, watching a deaf and dumb Olympics.

CHEESE-ROLLING RACE

Annual cheese-rolling races are held down the steep sides of Coopers Hill in Gloucestershire, as they have been since pagan times. The winners receive four kilogram (9 lb) Double Gloucester cheeses. In 1992, eight people were injured including one competitor who suffered a broken hip and head injuries.

EGG THROWING

The village of Aldbourne in Wiltshire stages a strange annual sporting event – a competition to throw a raw egg the greatest distance without breaking it. Competitors are allowed six hen's eggs, not more than two days old, and they throw the eggs onto the village green.

In 1990 the world record was broken at this event by Peter Keen, who threw his egg 87.14 m (285 ft 10¾ in) without breaking it. This shattered the previous record established in 1878 by the Australian Test cricketer R.F. 'Demon' Spofforth, who'd thrown a raw egg 45.7 m (150 ft).

OCTOPUSH

Octopush – underwater hockey – was devised in 1954 as a diversion for divers during their winter training. There are now more than 120 clubs around Britain and an international world championship.

A version of ice hockey, it features two teams of eight swimmers armed with wooden pushers, who try and flip the 'squid' – a 1.3 kg (3 lb) lead disc along the bottom of the swimming pool and into their opponent's goal. This consists of a 2.75 m (9 ft) gully protected by a sloping lip. Six swimmers are allowed into the water at any one time and three referees supervise play – two in the water and one at the poolside.

RECORD-BREAKING TEETH

Joe Ponder, from Love Valley, North Carolina, claims to have the world's strongest teeth; he was in the *Guiness Book of Records* until 1992. Joe was a professional boxer until he broke his neck – in a car accident. As therapy for his damaged muscles, Joe began lifting things and pulling things around with his teeth.

In 1973 he towed a 25,000 kg (55,000 lb) truck and a 42,000 kg (92,200 lb) rail car. In 1974 he lifted 180 kg (400 lb) and, on another occasion, Miss Nude America and Miss Nude World. In 1975 he hung by his teeth and went down a thirty-metre (100 ft) death-slide.

Joe, who stands 1.7 metres (5 ft 8 ins) tall, weighs ninety kilograms (200 lb) and has a sixty centimetre (24 in) diameter neck, has bent iron bars, lifted giant pumpkins and racing car engines, and hung from a helicopter.

He has fired 2,700 rounds per minute from a machine gun, and smashed cement blocks with a nine kilogram (20 lb) sledge hammer – all with his teeth.

TIGHTROPE-WALKING

Phillipe Petit is one of the world's great 'funambulists' – tightrope walker, to you.

In 1971 he walked between the towers of Notre Dame Cathedral in Paris and, two years later, successfully completed a wire-walk between the towers of the Sydney Harbour Bridge.

In 1974 he repeated the trick, only this time he was 1,350 feet-up, walking between the twin towers of the World Trade Center in New York. On reaching the ground he was arrested but his 'punishment' was to put on a tightrope show in Central Park. Ten thousand people turned up to watch.

 FACT The ability to fall asleep anywhere is coveted by many, but this is certainly no place to drop off, or for a somnambulist to take a nap.

Fame followed. He was offered a spot by the Ringling and Barnum Circus, and Bob Dylan wrote a song about him.

As part of the French Bicentennial celebrations in Paris in 1989, Petit walked along a 700-metre (2,300-ft) long cable, suspended 110 m (360 ft) above the ground, over the river Seine from the Palais de Chaillot on one bank to the second floor of the Eiffel Tower on the other. He wore a silver suit and buffalo skin slippers during the hour-long walk.

The greatest tightrope walker of them all was Charles Blondin (1824-1897). His most famous stunt was crossing the Niagara Falls, a feat he first did in 1859 and often repeated with more and more dangerous variations – blindfold, in a sack, trundling a wheelbarrow, on stilts, carrying a man on his back and sitting down midway to cook and eat an omelette.

He first appeared in London at the Great Exhibition in the Crystal Palace in London's Hyde Park in 1861. He is buried in Kensal Green cemetery in London.

'THE REGURGITATOR'

Stevie Starr is 'The Regurgitator', a man who travels the world for eleven months of the year getting paid to swallow things and bring them back up again.

He has swallowed fish, rings, snooker balls, flying bees, padlocks, light bulbs. He can swallow a pile of coins and count them in his stomach. He can swallow cigarette smoke, washing-up liquid and water and bring back a bubble full of smoke. He can also swallow a completed Rubik's cube and bring it up again with the sides moved.

MINE-BIKING

Local mountain bikers in Cornwall discovered a new challenge, racing through the underground tunnels of abandoned tin mines in the area, their progress lit only by lights on their bikes and on their helmets. This dangerous sport has now been abandoned; the pumps at the last working mine in Cornwall have been switched off and all the old mines are gradually flooding as a result.

CHANNEL-CROSSING

In a single week in 1981, the English Channel was crossed by seventeen swimmers, two blind water skiers, eighteen firemen in a rowing boat and eight Essex men on a raft powered by a combine harvester.

WADLOPEN

Wadlopen (walking on the *wad* or tide flat), a sport centred round Pieterbusen in the Netherlands, 320 km (200 miles) north east of Amsterdam, consists of walking fast between islands at low tide, in the months from May to September.

A *Wadlop*, according to one writer, is 'something like snow-shoeing on balloons made of yoghurt, only messier'.

WORM-CHARMING

The sport of worm charming dates back to the early 1980s when the first competitions were staged. Competitors are allocated a 1.2 x 0.9 m (4 ft x 3 ft) patch of ground and they have to coax as many earthworms out of the soil in fifteen minutes as they can.

A number of contestants have been banned for using washing-up liquid in their water – soap irritates a worm's skin and drives it to the surface – and now contestant are required to drink a sample of their charming water before play can commence. A variety of methods are allowed: using a spade or fork to agitate the soil, bagpipes and other musical instruments, folk dancing and other unlikely techniques.

RACES

In 1987 the Jockey Club disqualified a horse from a race that it had won at Ascot because it had eaten a Mars bar. The chocolate contained 'theobromine', a natural substance found in coffee beans, which is banned under club rules.

 Richard Carr from Dartmouth deploys a penny whistle and water gun when taking part in the Ninth Blackawton International Festival of Wormcharming in May 1992.

Rosie Ruiz came first in the 1979 New York marathon but was disqualified after someone gave evidence that she had taken the subway for part of the route. She finished first in the Boston marathon a year later but again was disqualified after a spectator reported she had joined the field a mile from the finish line.

In 1936 the famous black athlete, Jesse Owens, fresh from his gold medal triumphs at the 1936 Berlin Olympics, ran against and beat by nine and a half seconds, a famous horse of the day named McCall in a hundred yard (91.4 m) sprint.

Since then a number of athletes have attempted to emulate the feat, most recently, Daniel Sangouma, a French sprinter in October 1990. Sangouma stole an early lead on the horse named, Jappeloup in a race staged at the Saint Cloud racetrack near Paris, but was eventually beaten.

ROCK-HURLING

The annual Gotmaar Festival in Pandhura, India, is staged on the day after the September full moon. The 45,000 inhabitants of the town divide themselves into two groups, and start hurling rocks at each other until sunset when the fighting ends. In 1989 there were 616 casualties and four fatalities.

BASEBALL

A baseball travels nine per cent further in Denver than anywhere else into the US, according to US physicist Tom Stephen. Because the air in this high-altitude city is seventeen per cent thinner than at sea-level, balls will give hitters 0.003 seconds less time to strike them. However he also discovered that visiting teams adjust quickly to this situation.

STUNTS

A 1970s promotional stunt in the Idaho town of Castleford involved five people jumping into a 2,275 litres (600 gal) container of gooey lime-green gelatine to search for a marble at the bottom. The winner, David Barron, said, 'It was just like a dream I once had.'

Also in the 1970s, a man attempted to jump Minnesota's twelve-metre (40 ft) wide Lacque Park river on a power lawnmower. He missed by ten-and-a-half metres (35 ft).

John Evans is a builder from Derby who, in his spare time, specialises in balancing things on his head. These have included seventy-seven milk crates, sixty-three bricks, a sixty-eight-litre (18 gal) barrel of beer and two women, weighing around ninety-five kilograms (15 st).

FORTH BRIDGE

It is well-known that the job of painting the Forth Bridge never stops. It has passed into the language as symbolising a never-ending task. The area of steelwork to be painted covers an area of 170 hectares (145 acres).

GOLDEN GATE BRIDGE

One of the most impressive and famous bridges in the world is the Golden Gate Bridge which spans San Francisco harbour.

It was built by a man called Joseph Strauss, who had already built forty bridges in the jungles of Panama and a bridge across the Neva river in St Petersburg which the Bolsheviks used to storm the Tsar's winter palace during the Russian Revolution. The designer, Irving Morrow, was an architect of private homes who had never designed a bridge before.

Construction began in January 1933 and was completed four years later, at a cost of twenty-seven million dollars and the lives of eleven men.

The bridge contains 300,000 cu metres (389,000 cu yd) of concrete, 83,000 tonnes of structural steel and 80,000 tonnes of two-inch diameter wire. The colour of the bridge is called 'international orange'

On 27 May 1937 more than 200,000 people walked across the bridge for the first time. That afternoon, according to a report in the *San Francisco Chronicle*, the crowd tuned into 'one of the strangest symphonies the ear of man has ever heard. Above their heads hung four enormous harps, two from each of those lofty bridge towers. The towers were the pedestals of those harps, the deck their sounding board. And from those lofty instruments, the wind plucked melodies.'

The next day was the official opening. At noon, every foghorn, siren and church bell in the city sounded. Two ocean liners steamed underneath the bridge while 450 aeroplanes flew overhead.

In 1951, the bridge almost broke apart in a great storm. The roadway flexed by as much as 3.35 m (11 ft) and the main cables – normally eighty centimetres (32 in) apart – were rubbing together. Calculations done at the time showed that if the wind had lasted for just another twenty-five minutes, the bridge would have gone. As a result of this, 250 seven-tonne steel braces were placed under the road to strengthen it, at the cost of three million dollars and three lives.

MANCHESTER SHIP CANAL

The building of the Manchester Ship Canal was probably the most highly mechanised civil engineering project of the nineteenth century. More than 40,000,000 cu m (53½ million cu yd) was excavated, of which nine million (12 million) were sandstone rock.

Ten dredgers and ninety-seven steam excavators were used to accomplish the task; 173 locomotives and 6,300 trucks were used to remove spillage to the dumping grounds.

CHANNEL TUNNEL

The Channel Tunnel is the landmark project of twentieth century civil engineering, involving 14,000 workers and some extremely sophisticated tunnel-boring machines, used to remove several million metric tonnes of earth, rock and 'muck'.

Two of these huge cylindrical monsters, like giant worms, bored from opposite sides of the Channel. Each was guided along its path by a laser beam; on-board computers constantly checked the beam's position and angle and compared it with a three-dimensional map of the tunnel held in its memory.

WINCHESTER CATHEDRAL DIVER

Winchester Cathedral was saved from collapse by a deep-sea diver.

In 1905 the cathedral authorities discovered that the Medieval building was resting on tree trunks which, in turn, were lying on a waterlogged bed of peat. The pressure of the building – forty tonnes per square foot – was too much for these primitive foundations and the building would collapse unless it was made more secure.

As a result, William Walker was hired and, every day for nearly six years, he donned his ninety kilogram (200 lb) diving suit and climbed down into the watery pit where he dug away the peat and gradually replaced it with one million bricks, 115,000 concrete blocks and 25,000 sacks of concrete.

SAND CASTLES

Giant sand castles and sculptures have become all the rage in the US and Europe. One such construction, built by a team of two hundred volunteers was a replica of Bluebeard's castle. It measured thirteen metres (45 ft) high, forty metres

 The high tide advertised on the right could wash away these two beautiful sandcastle sculptures, so could a sudden gust of wind.

FACT The Great Pyramid at Giza sprawls across five hectares (13 acres) of desert. Long considered the tombs of pharaohs, little evidence of royal remains have been found in Egypt's eight pyramids (*see page 96*).

(130 ft) long and thirty metres (100 ft) wide and required 3,600 tonnes of sand and 2,5000 tonnes of water.

FLOATING HOTEL

The world's first floating hotel is moored forty miles off the coast of Western Australia on the edge of one of the great natural wonders of the world, the Great Barrier Reef.

The seven-storey hotel has two hundred bedrooms, three restaurants, two bars, sauna, library and gymnasium and a disco for up to four hundred guests. The eighty-two metre (270 ft) long, 12,000 tonne hotel is moored in position by seven anchors. It was built by an oil rig construction company in Singapore and then transported 4,800 km (3,000 miles) by sea on a special 'heavy lift' supertanker.

UNDERSEA HOTEL

Jules Undersea Lodge is five fathoms down in Bora Lagoon in the Florida Keys. A converted underwater research station, it can cater for six guests at a time who want to spend the night in rooms with private baths, or eat in the under-water restaurant. Giant portholes in each room allow you to count fish rather than sheep if you have problems sleeping.

EXCALIBUR HOTEL

The world's biggest hotel is now the Excalibur in Las Vegas, which opened its doors for the first time to paying guests in June 1990.

Designed like a Medieval castle, painted in pink, turquoise and gold, you could stay here for eleven years, change rooms every day, and never occupy the same room twice (there are 4,032).

There's a nightly, 'King Arthur's Tournament', the restaurant has Lance-a-Lotta Pasta on the menu, and the guests are entertained by jugglers and joust-ing knights.

WINCHESTER MYSTERY HOUSE

Sarah Winchester was the daughter-in-law of the man who made a twenty million-dollar fortune from the Winchester repeating rifle – 'the gun that won the West.'

When her daughter died at the age of six weeks and her husband at the age of forty-four, she consulted a spiritual medium in Boston. He told her that she was the victim of the vengeful spirits of America Indians killed by Winchester rifles. The only way she could placate them was to build a house and keep on building it, twenty-four hours a day, seven days a week. If she stopped, he told her, she would die.

So for thirty-eight years until she died at the age of eighty-two, Mrs Winchester supervised the construction of an extraordinary 160-room mansion, at San Jose, ninety kilometres (55 miles) south of San Francisco.

Designed to appease ghostly residents, the house has forty-seven chimneys to provide convenient escape routes for lost souls. A spider web motif recurs throughout the building as does the number thirteen – in rooms with thirteen windows, in chandeliers with thirteen lights, in stairways with thirteen steps.

There are staircases which lead nowhere and doors that give on to brick walls or dizzying drops. It is said that, around midnight you can hear the Lady of Mystery herself breathing heavily or playing the organ.

COUNCIL COTTAGE

Britain's tiniest council house is a circular thatched cottage, with one bedroom and a central fireplace, at Rayleigh in Essex.

Built in the eighteenth century, Dutch Cottage is considered suitable for two modern tenants; according to the 1831 census, it was home to brick maker, John Bright, his wife, Emma, their six children and a lodger.

EARTH HOUSES

Almost half the world's people live in buildings made of earth, mud and unbaked bricks.

In the Yemen there are mud buildings ten storeys high that have been continuously inhabited since the fourth century AD. Largest of all mud buildings is the Great Mosque in Djenné, in the West African country of Mali.

The advantages of earthen buildings are that they are well insulated against hot and cold weather and they are simple and cheap to construct and repair. The disadvantage is that they require constant maintenance.

Earth is now a fashionable building material in the US states of New Mexico, Arizona and southern California where it is known as adobe, a Spanish word for sun-dried earth.

BUNGALOW STONEHENGE

Eddie Prynne has constructed his own stone circle in the garden of his bungalow near St Austell. Mr Prynne was a quarryman until he lost the sight in one of his eyes following a mining accident. With time on his hands, he set out to indulge a lifetime-fascination with the neolithic 'cromlechs' he had seen on Bodmin Moor.

He now has nineteen stones weighing from two to ten tonnes in his garden. These include two one-tonne pieces of quartzite from Mount Pleasant in the Falkland Islands, shipped to him, free of charge by Sir Rex Hunt, the Island's former Governor. Eddie hopes to add a lump of chalk from the centre of the Channel Tunnel to his collection.

TRIANGULAR TOWER

One of the strangest follies in Britain is a triangular tower at Rushton in Northants built by Sir Thomas Tresham during The Reformation.

He received a secret and dangerous education as a Catholic during this fiercely Protestant era and became obsessed with codes, ciphers and the power of numbers.

Everything about the tower relates to the number three – a homage to the Trinity. It is three-sided and three-storeyed, with triangular or hexagonal rooms decorated with trefoils or triangles in groups of three. There are Latin inscriptions, each with thirty-three letters and other seemingly endless variations on the same theme.

PRIVATE PYRAMID

Jim Onan of Wadsworth, Illinois, has built his very own, five-storey-high, gold-plated pyramid to live in. It is surrounded by a shark-filled moat. It has five bedrooms, six bathrooms, seven fireplaces and an observatory on the top floor.

NEWGRANGE

Seven centuries older than the pyramids and older by far than Stonehenge, Newgrange is the oldest man-made structure in Europe. Built 5,000 years ago and situated fifty kilometres (30 miles) north of Dublin, it is a vast, impressive and mysterious house of the dead.

Constructed from more than 550 huge slate slabs, each weighing more than a ton, it is covered by a grass-topped cairn weighing 200,000 tonnes which contains a million sack-fulls of stone that took one thousand labourers thirty years to build.

At dawn on the winter solstice, the sun's rays shine through an aperture, travel down an eighteen-metre (60 ft) passageway into the cruciform central chamber and illuminate it for seventeen minutes with a golden light.

HAND-BUILT CATHEDRAL

An ex-priest named Justo Gallego has spent more than thirty years using damaged building materials to construct his own personal monument to God, a thousand-seater cathedral overlooking Majorade del Campo, a small town twenty-five kilometres (15 miles) east of Madrid in Spain. The eccentric building looks like castle with it's two, fifty-five metre (180 ft) towers. The roof is of zinc and the entrance is based on that of the White House in Washington DC.

ROLLER-COASTERS

Roller-coasters originated in Russia and were originally called 'Russian Mountains.' First made in the seventeenth century, they had no wheels and passengers sped down icy slopes on sleds.

The French added wheels to this amusement ride in 1804 and the first commercial roller-coaster was built in 1884, at New York's Coney Island, by an inventor named LaMarcus A.Thompson, known as the 'Father of Gravity'.

SKYSCRAPERS

The World Trade Center in New York City contains enough concrete to run a 1.5m (5 ft) wide path from New York to Washington DC, and enough electrical wire to reach Mexico City.

It has its own zip codes (10047 and 10048), twenty local bank branches and food service for 20,000 at a sitting. When the sun shines, the glass from the aluminium-clad towers can be seen two states away.

One Shell Plaza in Houston, which at the time it was built was the tallest building west of the Mississippi, had twenty-six lift cars with walls 2.7m (9 ft) high – all covered in real leather.

The architect wanted no seams or joints in the leather, so they had to search the world to find some herds of nine-foot cows. They eventually found

 The twin towers of the World Trade Center still dominate the New York skyline, but the tallest building in the world is now the Sears Tower in Chicago.

them in Holland and Belgium. The leather cost $1,915 at the time, about $50,000 in all.

The walls became so smothered in carved graffiti that the leather had to be replaced every six months.

Mitsui, the Japanese construction firm, has plans to build the world's first super-sky scraper as the centrepiece of a new circular city, fourteen kilometres (8.7 miles) in diameter, called simply, 'Mother'.

The central tower would be 220-storeys high reaching almost 900m (3,000 ft) into the atmosphere. Conical foundations more than 185 m (600 ft) deep would be needed to anchor it. It would take an estimated seventeen years and $300 billion to build.

The tallest building between Frankfurt and Singapore is the 175 m (575 ft) high Metropol Tower in Mersin, Turkey's third-largest port.

MOHAWK BUILDERS

Since the 1920s, the majority of New York's sky scrapers and bridges have been built with the help of Mohawk Indians from a small reservation near Montreal. The reason is they have no fear of heights.

BERLIN WALL

The Berlin Wall, the physical symbol of the Cold War between East and West, ran for 160 km (100 miles), encircling West Berlin. Building began on Sunday 13 August, 1961 and it stood until 1989/1990, when the world changed.

The Wall actually consisted of nine distinct lines of obstacles, ninety metres (300 ft) wide. The wall itself was 4.5 m (15 ft) high, smooth and topped by a slippery, thirty -eight centimetre (15 in) diameter pipe on which it was impossible to get a grip.

Other obstacles included two, 1.5 metre (5 ft) high fences, wired to set

 The concrete part of the Iron Curtain, the Berlin Wall, was pulled down in November 1989. A month earlier, the human wrecking balls would have been shot.

off alarms at a touch, trip wires fixed to flare launchers, an anti-vehicle trench, a dog-run, patrolled by a total of 274 Alsatians, concrete watchtowers with searchlights and machine guns, a perimeter road patrolled by armoured personnel carriers and guards, anti-personnel mines hidden in grass and steel spikes buried in ploughed earth.

In the first twenty-one years of the Wall, 186,868 people escaped from the East to the West, 38,260 of them directly over the wall or via the East-West German border.

The Wall has now virtually disappeared. Much of it was used as hardcore for building roads. Sections covered in graffiti were carved up and sold by the East German government to art dealers. Five pieces reached between £12-17,000 each at a dealer's in London's Mayfair.

WALLED CITY

The old Walled City of Kowloon in Hong Kong – known locally as *Hak Nam*, the city of darkness – is being demolished. It was the biggest slum in the world. One writer described it as the world's longest lasting, largest, most lawless, most dangerous, and most overcrowded squat.

Covering 2.6 hectares (6 1/2 acres) of solid buildings, it was home to 33,000 people and used to be divided by two warring Triad factions – the 'Ging Wu' and the '14K'.

FIRSTS

The world's first robot-shaped building houses the Bank of Asia in Bangkok. It cost eight million pounds.

The world's first rotating house was completed in 1984 by a French inventor, M. Francois Labbé, in the village of Saint-Isidore, near Nice. Constructed entirely of metal, it can be turned to face the sun or the shade at the press of a button. Talk about all mod cons!

ONE WONDER

Six of the Seven Wonders of the Ancient world have fallen – either as a result of neglect, vandals, earthquakes or wars. Only the Great Pyramid still stands.

SEVEN FUTURE WONDERS

The Tokyo-based Mitsubishi Research Institute announced its plan in 1983 to try and raise £400 billion to build the Seven Wonders of the Modern World.
The Wonders were:

✪ A super highway linking Europe and China, running from London to Peking.

✪ An underwater tunnel joining Europe and Africa at Gibraltar.

✪ A huge lake in central Africa, produced by damming the Congo River.

✪ A second canal across central America.

✪ A third canal across Malaysia, which would cut the sailing distance from the Far East to the Indian Ocean by more than 2,250 km (1,400 miles).

✪ Vast irrigation projects to turn the Saharan and Arabian deserts green.

✪ A trillion-pound solar energy plant on the Equator.

THE HOUSTON ASTRODOME

The Houston Astrodome was the world's first domed stadium and the world's biggest air-conditioned room. The man behind it, Judge Roy Hofheinz, a two-term mayor of Houston, got the idea from studying the Coliseum in Rome. He said: 'We'll build a stadium that will make Emperor Titus' playhouse look like an abandoned brickyard.'

The dome was built on former swamp land and it took three million dollars, just to drain the site and a further \$31.6 million and nine years to complete the colossal structure.

It stands sixty metres (208 ft) high, is 800 m ($1/2$ ml) in diameter and covers 3.8 hectares (9 $1/2$ acres). The score-board inside is four storeys high, cost two million dollars to construct and is run by eight technicians.

In the roof, Hofheinz built himself a special 'dome home' featuring a shooting gallery, an Astroturf putting green, a pseudo-Gothic chapel, a presidential suite in the style of Louis XIV and a bar called the Tipsy Tavern (it has a slanted floor).

Hofheinz died in 1982 and his personal suite, visited by, Elvis Presley, Lyndon Johnson and the Duke of Windsor among others is to be demolished to make way for an additional 15,000 seats.

VENDING MACHINES

Japan has more vending machines per capita than any other country in the world. In 1977 there were 3.2 million – one for every thirty-six people. By 1990, there were five million, one for every twenty-three people.

The machines sell golf balls, fish burgers, panty-hose, bags of rice, cans of coffee, condoms, phone cards, batteries, hot spring water, beef, floppy discs, cut flowers, tickets, hot noodles, hamburgers, popcorn, cold chocolate, milk-shakes, whisky, rice balls, whiffs of oxygen. Eleven thousand of them sell porno-graphic magazines. They also dispense Bibles, fishing bait, two-litre kegs of sake, insurance and incense.

A single vending machine consumes more electricity than an average one-fam-ily dwelling. Food and drink machines (which account for more than half the

 An up–market vending machine at a Paris Metro station offers an inedible alternative to the normal drinks and chocolates – ten different sizes of Levi 501 jeans.

country's vending machines) consume the equivalent of the entire output of a nuclear plant.

In recent years, three American servicemen have been killed and twelve others have suffered injuries ranging from a broken toe to a coma after vending machines fell on them at military bases in Europe and Korea.

The machines dispensed cold drinks and weighed up to 450 kg (1,000 lb). The accidents happened because servicemen had discovered that if you rocked the machine at an angle, it was possible to get a free can. What they didn't realise is that these machines dispense the cans by gravity and therefore stores them near the top and towards the front of the machine. When tipped forward as little as twenty degrees, the machine can topple over.

MUSEUMS

The Mutter Museum in Chicago was founded in 1858 and remains unchanged from its Victorian heyday. It houses a collection of more than 20,000 bizarre medical artefacts including antique instruments, preserved pathological specimens, examples of rare anatomical anomalies and other medical curiosities.

These include a tonsil guillotine, a 370-gm (13 oz) bladder stone, a range of trepanned skulls from Peru and the skeleton of a 2.3 metre (7 ft 6s in) Kentucky giant.

There is also a collection of 3,000 objects that people have swallowed or inhaled including ammunition, toy opera glasses and a small metal battleship.

England's first chimney pot museum has been set up by farmer, Chris Fookes at Milton Abbas in Dorset.

The New York State Museum of Cheese has been established in Rome, a town that was the site of America's first cheese factory, built by Jesse Williams in

1851. The local mayor hopes it will attract tourists and says he intends to 'milk the idea for all it's worth.'

Robert Opie started his collection of packaging with the wrapper from a tube of Munchies when he was sixteen. He now has more than one million objects in his Museum of Advertising and Packaging in Gloucester which he set up in 1984. He is the proud owner of 10,000 yoghurt pots.

According to a report from Britain's National Audit Office, less than half of the objects in Britain's major museums are on display, due to lack of space.

The National Portrait Gallery, for instance, has 9,000 works in its collection and 2,250 on display. The Tate owns 54,394 works and displays just over 2,000. The British Museum has four million objects in its collection but only 23,225 sq m (250,000 sq ft) in which to display them.

FAKE PETS

Japanese toy makers have developed 'fake pets' for lonely people. The first of these is 'Mew', a stuffed toy cat with an electronic sensor built in, that purrs when it is stroked.

Another company, Nomura Toys, produce 'Super Doggy Guard One', a mechanical dog with an infra red sensor, that barks when anything moves.

Yet another company sells a puppy with a voice-recognition device that yelps and wags its tail when you call its name.

TEDDY BEARS

The history of the Teddy Bear dates from around 1902 when the first of these cuddly toys were sold in both Germany and America.

In the US, it all began with the birth of a popular legend. President Teddy Roosevelt was on a hunting trip and, so the story went, refused to shoot a captured bear cub.

The truth of the matter was slightly different and can be found in the *Washington Post* for Saturday 15 November 1902, under the headline, 'One Bear Bagged'.

It seems that the President and his hunting party used their dogs to chase a big black bear weighing 105 kg (235 lb) for many miles and many hours until it was exhausted. They cornered it, knocked it unconscious and roped it to a tree. When the President caught up with them, he refused to shoot the bear. (The bear was, in fact, killed with a knife).

The story grew (or shrank) in the telling and became the subject of a political cartoon. At every re-telling the bear became more cub-like and more appealing.

`Rose and Morris Michtom were aware of the public interest and made two bears which they put in their shop window in Brooklyn, New York. Demand was such that Morris shrewdly wrote to the President to get his permission to call them 'Teddy Bears'. By 1907, the Michtom's had become so successful, they moved to larger premises and became the Ideal Toy and Novelty Company, which still thrives to this day.

The German side of the story is more straight forward. Margaret Steiff (b. 1847) contracted polio as a child and began making stuffed toys for sale in her neighbourhood. Her nephew Richard, an artist with a keen interest in bears, persuaded her to make a stuffed bear toy and it was an immediate hit.

The technical term for an obsession with Teddy Bears is 'arctophilia', from *arctos* the Greek for bear. Obsessives are also known as 'bearaholics'.

STRANGE BUYS

International Information Service Ltd is a London-based company that has a network of shoppers in 128 countries who scour supermarket shelves for innovative products. They also buy established goods and send them to company laboratories for testing, to maintain quality control.

Some of the more unusual products they have located are: American tubes of mashed potatoes called *Ketchips* that have a tomato ketchup centre; Finnish nappies that turn urine into gel; *Le Pooch* cologne for dogs; black spaghetti from Japan, made from seaweed; monkey-gland burgers from South Africa; an Israeli body deodorant that claims to keep you odour-free for five to eight months; a fish food that turns your goldfish a darker shade of gold.

The company also maintains a 'Black Museum' of products with unfortunate names. These include: *Mukk* yoghurt and *Mental* breath fresheners from Italy, *Homo Sausage* salami and *Cow* shaving foam from Japan; *Bums* biscuits and *Fartek* baby wear from Sweden; and *Plopp* chocolate bars from Germany.

A Japanese firm has sold 400,000 pairs of 'insecticide tights'. These are designed to be lethal to spiders and cockroaches that are increasingly infesting the country's offices.

The Fossil Shop in Lyme Regis in Dorset sells genuine 140-million-year-old dinosaur-dung bookends.

Sweet Art in Kansas City have developed a new system for decorating cakes with photographs or logos. It uses a personal computer, a video camera, a robot arm and a sonar-controlled table to do the job.

HOLOGRAPHIC CHOCOLATE

The Dimensional Foods Corporation of Boston, founded in 1987, have patented a process for putting holograms on chocolate and other foods. They are also working on an experimental lollipop which shows animated cartoons when it is twirled.

DUBIOUS DUST

Gordon Bennett & Associates Inc of Palo Alto California market a 'wine dust'

to sprinkle on bottles to make them look old. A spokesman for the company claims that the dust contains 'forty-two mysterious ingredients' including 'belly-button lint tweezered out of the statue of the Venus de Milo.'

ZIPPO

Every ship in the Royal Navy, most army units and half of the RAF squadrons have customised Zippo lighters.

SHOPPING TROLLEYS

The shopping trolley now ranks as one of the world's most frequently-used four-wheel devices, second only to the automobile.

It was first developed by Sylvan Goldman, a grocery store owner from Oklahoma, who noticed that housewives stopped shopping when their bags got too heavy. By the time he died in 1984 he had made a $400 million fortune. At one point there was so much demand for his 'shopping carts' that there was a seven-year waiting list for delivery.

The shopping trolley first appeared in the UK in 1950 at Sainsbury's in Croydon. An average-sized supermarket now has a fleet of 250 trolleys. Between fifteen and twenty-five per cent of these disappear every year and cost around seventy-two pounds each to replace.

According to the Royal Society for the Prevention of Accidents, in 1991 some 7,500 people were injured after tangling with shopping trolleys.

SUPERMARKETS

Depending on which authority you believe, the world's first supermarket was either: the Alpha Beta Food market in Pomona; the World's Grocerteria in Ocean Park; the Big Bear Market in Elizabeth, New Jersey; the Piggly Wiggly store in Memphis, Tennessee; the Ralph Store on Spring Street in downtown Los Angeles;

or King Kullen on Long Island, New York.

PEARLS

Pearls are formed in oysters when a grain of sand or a tiny sea creature becomes trapped in the fleshy parts and is embalmed in a secretion of tiny calcium carbonate crystals, similar to the mother-of-pearl that coats the shell. They are also found in other molluscs, including the conch, which produces a very rare pink pearl.

The ancients were puzzled by them. One theory was that they were caused by lightning penetrating the oyster. Pliny believed they were 'hardened raindrops fallen into basking oysters.'

The Chinese were the first to try to produce pearls artificially, in the thirteenth century, by persuading mussels to coat mud pellets with 'nacre' (mother-of-pearl). But it was a former Japanese noodle-peddler, named Kokitichi Mikimoto who perfected the technique after experimenting for twenty years with a group of marine biologists.

Japan now has more than three hundred sea farms producing these 'cultured' pearls. They are produced by surgically implanting a small mother-of-pearl bead in the oyster, using a gold-tipped instrument. The oysters then recuperate in wire cages suspended from wooden rafts in calm bays. They are later x-rayed to make sure the nucleus has been retained.

A pearl's iridescent quality, known as 'lustre' or 'orient' is produced by the scattering of light between the layers of transparent nacre. Pearls come in many colours – blue, yellow, mauve, cream and black.

Black pearls, the most expensive and rarest of all, are in fact various shades of grey, the most valuable having a greenish tinge.

In 1917, the famous jeweller, Pierre Cartier exchanged a two-strand necklace of black pearls for a five-storey Renaissance mansion on Fifth Avenue, which is still used as the company's New York premises.

There is an age-old saying that pearls like to be worn; they lose their lustre if neglected.

FANTASTIC INVENTIONS!

SPRINGWALKER

A Californian company called Applied Motion, has invented a contraption called a 'Springwalker' – a twenty-five kilogram (55 lb), skeletal arrangement of levers and stilts, which the wearer straps himself into and then bounces along by pumping his or her feet. This stretches and relaxes in turn a bungee-cord, mounted behind the operator's back. A spring absorbs the shock waves and cushions the rider.

The inventors claim that the Springwalker lengthens your stride, doubles your leverage and recovers eighty per cent of vertical energy; by comparison, kangaroos, the most efficient animal hoppers, can only recover forty per cent.

A lightweight, ten-kilogram (22-lb) sports model the company is developing should bounce the rider along at forty kilometres per hour (25 mph) – the average speed Carl Lewis reaches over one hundred metres.

VEG-HEADS

US Patent No. 4,827,666, filed in 1989, is for a range of plastic moulds that give vegetables a strange appearance.

Richard Twedell III experimented by growing vegetables in bottles and discovered they assumed the shape of their containers. His invention consists of two, clear plastic moulds that turn vegetables like squash, cucumbers, pumpkins and egg plants, into strange-looking characters.

NOSE-PICKER

Since 1919, more than a dozen patents have been filed at the US Patent Office for nose-picking devices. These include a 1924 'nasal-cleaning device', which consists of a brush with soft, rubber blades.

MOUSE TRAPS

Britain's biggest selling mouse trap is the wooden spring-trap, baited with cheese. The 'Little Nipper', of which a million are sold every year was invented by James Henry Atkinson and has been manufactured by the family firm of Proctor Bros in South Wales since 1875. One customer in Australia used it to trap a forty-six centimetre (18-in) tiger snake.

The firm is establishing the world's second mousetrap museum; the first is in Hamelin, the German town featured in the famous Pied Piper poem.

Its earliest relic is a replica of a 3,000 year-old clay trap from an Egyptian tomb, left to prevent mice eating either the food left for the deceased on its journey to the hereafter or the mummy itself.

Medieval moneylenders in Europe were particularly keen on using traps to prevent mice eating their customers' paper pledges.

 FACT Tampering with nature can be fun when you can grow vegetables in your own image. Place them in a two-part plastic mould of your own head.

German industrialist, Rheinhard Hellwig from Dusseldorf has the biggest collection in the world, of more than 1,000 traps. He also has nearly 2,000 trap patents on a computer database.

The traps employ a wide variety of techniques: hinged metal traps, 'deadfall' traps that slam shut, guillotines, electric traps and one which has a bridge over a bucket of water that collapses when a mouse tries to walk over it.

He paid nearly one thousand dollars for a 'mirror' trap, patented by George Walker in Pennsylvania in 1871. The mouse enters the trap, sees itself in the mirror and thinks it has competition for the lump of cheese. It lunges for the bait and gets speared in the process.

Mr Hellwig is writing a book on mousetraps with David Drummond, a retired civil servant, who has become the world's leading authority on the subject as a result of his former career. He worked on rodent and pest control for the UN Food and Agriculture Organisation.

A new electronic trap, 'Mouse Alert', was launched in 1992 and aimed at companies with sensitive computers or valuable stock.

When the mouse enters the box-like trap, it intercepts two infra-red beams – one slides the doors shut at each end, the other sends a signal to a central computer which alerts patrolling pest-control officers.

Four thousand patents for variations on the mousetrap have been registered since the first US mousetrap patent was issued in 1838. Between fifty and one hundred new designs come in to the US Patent Office every year; sixty-five to seventy per cent are sufficiently different to be eligible for patent protection.

CAT FLAPS

Sir Isaac Newton is credited with inventing the cat flap, but the essential idea pre-dates him. The fourteenth century poet, Geoffrey Chaucer refers to a hole cut in the door for the family cat in *The Miller's Tale*.

CAT'S EYES

'Cat's eyes' – reflector studs set in the middle of the road – were invented by an Englishman, Percy Shaw. Though he became a millionaire, he lived a simple life in a house beside his factory in Yorkshire. He had no carpet in his living room, so he could throw onto the floor the continuous stream of matches he used to light his pipe, (which he filled with broken-up cigars). He died in 1976, aged eighty-six.

MACKINTOSH

The mackintosh is so called (though wrongly spelled) after its inventor, Charles Macintosh, a Scotsman who was one of the pioneers of the chemical industry. Charles was born in 1766, and was brought up at his father's fortress-like dye-making works. The factory and the workers' houses were surrounded by a three metre (10 ft) wall. The workers were all Gaelic-speaking Highlanders who lived under a regime of military discipline. Thus were early industrial secrets preserved. Charles patented his waterproof fabric in 1823 and advertised the raincoats as 'life preservers' for stage coach drivers, horsemen, mariners and others who had to face the rigours of the weather.

EAR MUFFS

Chester Greenwood, who invented the ear muff in 1877, also held 125 other patents, including such devices as a spring-tooth rake, aeroplane shock absorbers and self-priming spark plugs.

To celebrate the centenary of his most famous invention, his hometown of Farmington, Maine built a pair of giant ear muffs as big as automobile tyres and mounted them on a municipal fire truck. They also staged an ear muff fashion show, a 'longest ears' competition and a foot race to the former site of Greenwoood's Ear Protector Factory which, at the time of the inventor's death in 1937, was producing millions of ear muffs a year and was operating twenty-four hours a day.

ELECTROLUBE

'Electrolube', a synthetic lubricant that is resistant to both extremes of cold and heat, was invented in 1956 by Henry Kingsbury. Used in both the early US space rockets and in the Paris metro, Electrolube has also been used to remove chewing gum from carpets and restore the quality of scratched, (78 rpm) records.

MARGARINE

Margarine is the invention of Mége-Mouries, a French scientist, who was working in response to the urgent call of Napoleon III to find a substitute for butter. What the inventor did was to 'short-circuit' the cow. The cow makes milk, and we make butter from the milk fat. Mége-Mouries, however, took the fat and turned it directly into margarine.

The name comes from the Greek word for a pearl; the millions of little globules of fat that formed in the manufacturing process, reminded the inventor of pearls. Mége-Mouries patented his process in 1874.

INVENTORS

Mr George Rhodes, former secretary of the Society of Inventors in Manchester, has invented, among other useful devices, an open-ended trouser rack, a roulette dart board and a warm toilet seat cover, which folds away and can be carried in a handbag.

The safety pin was invented in three hours by Walter Hunt in 1849, to pay off a debt of fifteen dollars.

The first video game system was patented in April 1972 by Ralph Baer, (an engineer with a New Hampshire defence contractor) and his colleagues.

 Actress Hedy Lamarr was one of the world's most glamorous and beautiful inventors. Her movies must have had some very deep sub–plots.

 Cat's–eyes inventor, Percy Shaw, with his ever–present pipe, enjoyed the simple, homely pleasures of life. For him, all the glory was reflected.

Ten year-old Clint Lenz earned himself first place in the national, 'Invent America' competition in 1992 with his luminous lavatory seat. It is now installed as an exhibit in the Smithsonian Institution.

HEATH ROBINSON

William Heath Robinson's father and two brothers were all illustrators for magazines and newspapers. He began his career as a serious illustrator but, when his publisher went bankrupt and times were tight, he turned to humorous work – particularly the unnecessarily complex and strange machinery for doing extraordinary tasks – that are now forever associated with his name.

Inventions like: *A unique contraption for blowing out the candle when the dressing table is a long way from the bed.*

A planned Heath Robinson museum in London will feature a house in which the kitchen has a live chicken which lays eggs in a tube that carries them straight into a saucepan. The bedroom will have a pulley which dangles screaming babies out of the window and the dining-room will turn upside down to form a spare bedroom.

HEDY LAMARR

Actress Hedy Lamarr, the famous MGM starlet and *femme fatale*, was also a secret inventor. In June 1941, she and composer, George Antheil patented a classified communication system, especially suitable for submarines. The essence of the device is that it changes radio frequencies intermittently and simultaneously between the transmitter and receiver, thus defeating any attempt by an enemy to monitor the signals.

'Q'

Q, the secret-gadget-devisor in Ian Fleming's James Bond adventures, was partly based on the skilful Charles Fraser-Smith, who died in November 1992.

Fraser-Smith worked for the secret services during the war producing objects such as dominoes, hairbrushes and shaving brushes, modified to hold maps or escape-files, as well as tiny Minox cameras and minute telescopes disguised as nicotine-stained cigarette-holders.

ACCIDENTAL INVENTIONS

A French chemist named, Henri Moissan was trying to manufacture artificial diamonds; in the process he accidentally discovered the compound, calcium carbide. When combined with water it was found to produce a burnable gas – acetylene. This became the most common form of lighting until the invention of the electric light bulb.

A German chemist, Fritz Klatte tried to develop an aircraft varnish using acetylene. In 1912 he created a combination which turned out to be the world's first plastic – vinyl chloride.

PATENTS

The Science Reference Library, just off London's Chancery Lane, holds all the patents for the British Patent Office, to which it is attached. When they counted the patents on the shelves and in the vaults in December 1983, staff reported a total of 2,624,176 British Patents and 20,375,824 foreign patents. By 1987, the figure was 30 million.

Patents stored there include:

✪ A 1970 patent, filed by British Rail for a flying saucer powered by thermonuclear fusion.

✪ An unusual method of stopping a car dead in its tracks, filed by Tai Tung Wong of Hong Kong – an anchor dropped in the road.

✪ An invention to trick a burglar into triggering a smoke cartridge which fills the room with a cloud so thick, the intruder can't find anything to steal, or the way to get out.

✪ A United Kingdom Atomic Energy Authority (UKAEA) patent for a steam-powered tea-making machine.

Nothing of substance in a patent can be changed once it's been published. If you are granted a patent you gain a limited monopoly on the idea for a maximum of twenty years. The monopoly ends when a patent expires or is revoked by a court of law. Unlike books, patents remain permanently in print.

Thomas Edison filed 1,093 patents, most of them successful, in his long career of invention.

About 1,200 new American patents are issued each Tuesday at noon. More than four million have been issued since the US Patent Office began in 1790.

Unusual inventions registered at the US Patent Office include a strip of silk tape to prevent breathing through the mouth, registered in 1920 by Richard Jefferies, a design to 'harmonise facial features'; a tongue shield which fits like a sock, designed to stop the taste of unpleasant medicines; and a machine designed in 1929 to produce artificial dimples in the cheeks with the aid of three bullet-shaped screws.

Richard Szauer Jr of Oberlingen in West German, filed a European patent in eleven countries to protect his invention – an oversize inflatable thumb, for hitchhikers who can't get lifts.

In 1981, the Japanese company, Sony was granted a US patent for a 'gramo-car' – a toy car which runs round a LP record, tracking the groove with a hidden stylus and producing the sound through a built-in amplifier and loudspeaker.

Among the bizarre inventions patented in Britain in Edwardian times were: Leder's Foul Breath Indicator, a curved tube linking mouth and nose allowing 'any foulness or unpleasant state of the breath [to] be readily detected by the sense of smell'; Jephson's Improved Coffin for Indicating the Burial Alive of a Person In A Trance; and – for circus manager's – Wulff's Improved Apparatus for Throwing Animals in the Air for Exhibition Purposes.

CARS

The name, Volvo comes from the Latin meaning 'I roll'. The Volvo emblem is the old chemical symbol for iron.

The Cadillac is named after the founder of Detroit, Antoine de la Mothe Cadillac.

The Audi name has an interesting history. The company was started in 1899 by Dr August Horch who began building cars bearing his name. However he was, by all accounts a difficult man and he fell out with his original backers and left to start another company. As a result of the dispute he was unable to continue using his own name for the cars he built . *Horch* in German means 'hear' so he used the Latin translation for this – *audi*.

 The stretch cadillac can cause problems for a back seat driver. Here, a passenger is making a long distance telephone call to the chauffeur.

 A Finnish advertising vehicle – a mechanical clockwork orange, which runs on 5–star Jaffa. No doubt, it would cause a most unusual traffic jam.

Charles Rolls, co-founder of the Rolls-Royce company, died in 1910 at the age of thirty-three. He was Britain's first aviation fatality, having crashed his Wright biplane while competing in an air show at Bournemouth.

French racing driver, Jean Behra always kept a spare, plastic right ear in his pocket. He'd lost his original in an accident in 1955.

Many terms connected with the car derive from French. *Chauffeur*, for instance, is the French translation of the word for 'stoker' and derives from the early days of steam-powered vehicles which required someone to tend the boiler.

Limousine is derived from the protective cloak worn by shepherds in the Limousin district of France and was used to describe a car fully enclosed from the elements.

The term 'pits' in racing derives from the 1908 French Grand Prix in Dieppe, when mechanics literally dug pits beside the track in order to service the cars from underneath.

The fictional car 'Chitty-Chitty-Bang-Bang' was based on a real car of that name, owned and raced at the old Brooklands track by Count Louis Zborowski.

The Batmobile also existed for real. It was the name of a 1955 Lincoln Futura.

The most luxurious customised car in the world may be the 'Hollywood Dream', a fifty-seater twenty-two wheeled customised Cadillac bought second-hand in Australia for 750,000 US dollars in 1988 by Kenji Kawamuda, owner of a sports and fitness centre near Osaka, Japan.

Powered by an eight-litre engine, the car is twenty metres (66 ft) long and contains inside it a bedroom that sleeps four, a cinema, a cocktail bar and a tv lounge. Outside it carries a small swimming pool, a hot tub and a one-hole golf course.

The Renault Zoom is an electric car that may prove to be answer to city transport and parking problems. Its full length is 2.6 m (8 ft 6 in) but, if the parking place is too small, it simply tucks up its rear wheels and makes itself almost two feet shorter. The power for the two-seater comes from nickel cadmium batteries that give a range of 150 km (95 miles) around-town and speeds up to 120 km per hour (75 mph).

In a few years time the first hydrogen-powered cars will be road-tested. The Japanese company Mazda has already built prototypes which have achieved speeds of 145 km per hour (90 mph) and travelled 200 km (125 miles). The advantage of such cars is that the fuel can be extracted from water. After combustion, the fuel returns to water, making them pollution-free.

One of the highlights of the 'Car 91' exhibition at Wembley Exhibition Centre in London was a thirty-six-speaker car stereo system fitted in a Mazda van. It produced a sound ten times louder than *Concorde* and cost at least £45,000.

There are about six hundred car designers in Europe.

SECRET COLLECTION

The largest and most extraordinary collection of automobiles in the world was assembled by two brothers Fritz and Hans Schlumpf under equally extraordinary circumstances.

The Swiss brothers inherited a textile business, in the French region of Alsace, which they ran for forty years. What none of the workers knew was that the brothers were secretly building-up a huge car collection in one of their abandoned textile factories in the middle of the city of Mulhouse.

Prize automobiles, purchased from all over the world, were brought to the plant at night on special train. The secret was shared by only a handful of trusted insiders and no one was allowed to see the collection for many years, except the brothers themselves, who established it as a tribute to their mother to whom they were both devoted.

When business went from bad to worse and the company went bankrupt in 1976, workers broke into the plant to discover the vast collection of more than 600 luxury cars – Bugattis, Rolls Royces, Mercedes, Alfa Romeos and Bentleys among them – arranged in a splendid setting, illuminated by antique gas lamps.

The brothers avoided legal problems by escaping to Switzerland. The huge collection is now owned by the city of Mulhouse and continues to attract hundreds of thousands of visitors a year. The two bothers, broken-hearted at the loss of their treasures, died in 1989 and 1992.

ROYAL ROLLERS

Some of the most ornate and expensive Rolls-Royces ever built were exported to India in the years leading up to independence in 1947, to satisfy the whims of the wealthy Maharajahs. More than a thousand of these cars were exported and then customised in extraordinary ways.

The Maharajah of Patiala was a bulk- buyer who owned no less than thirty-eight. Another Maharajah had eight in his garage, which could accommodate 450 cars.

The Maharajah of Nabha had his car customised in the shape of a swan. The exhaust fumes were discharged through the bird's beak.

The Maharajah of Patiala had his Rolls-Royce painted salmon-pink with satin upholstery to match. The car's diamond-studded dashboard was so valuable that it had to be protected by four armed guards every time it went in for a service. Another maharajah had his encrusted with mother of pearl and christened it Pearl of the East.

The Rolls' reputation for reliability led to their being used in rugged mountain terrain and many were converted for use on tiger hunts. They incorporated searchlights, gun racks and steps for bearers to stand on during shoots.

The Nawab of Bahawalpur had his converted into an armoured car with gun turret.

In recent years, an estimated three-quarters of these magnificent vehicles have been smuggled illegally out of India and sold to collectors in the West for high prices.

GOLDMOBILE

There were four identical cars made for the James Bond movie, *Goldfinger* – two were used in the movie and two for promotional tours. Two other one-third-scale models were also built; one was given to Prince Andrew, the other to Prince Reza, son of the former Shah of Iran.

AUTO-ART

A replica of Stonehenge has been built by a retired engineer named James Reinders, in a field outside the town of Alliance in the US state of Nebraska, out of twenty-two automobiles from the sixties and seventies. 'Carhenge' is, depending on your point of view, an artwork or an elaborate joke.

Reinder has suggested that what is needed to complement this work is a Leaning Tyre of Pisa, made of tractor tyres.

Apart from the original monument, his inspiration for Carhenge was an earlier work called 'Cadillac Ranch', built by a Texan millionaire called, Stanley Marsh III. This consists of twelve Cadillacs, buried nose-down in a row, at the same angle as the Egyptian Pyramids.

Other controversial 'car-art' works include: a twenty metre (65 ft) high stack of cars encased in concrete, built by a French sculptor named Arman, and installed at the Montcel museum park in Paris; the 'Golden Bird', a golden-winged Ford Fiesta created by 'action artist' H.A.Schult which nests on the tower of the city museum in Cologne, Germany. Schult has also created artworks with Ford cars set in blocks of marble and ice.

TIME-CAPSULE GARAGES

A German businessman has discovered a lucrative business – time-capsule garages, where proud owners of rare cars can store their treasures in cocooned splendour. The cars are packed in air-tight plastic covers and a vacuum pump is used to suck out the air. The wrapped car is then packed in a box which is nailed down tightly. This system claims to keep the car free from rust and mildew until it is unwrapped at some stage in the future.

CRASHES

In 1974, the US reduced its upper speed limit to fifty-five miles per hour. The death toll on the roads was immediately halved as a result.

Road deaths in Germany increased by eighteen per cent when the country abolished speed limits on its autobahns.

At forty miles per hour, eighty five per cent of pedestrians hit by cars die; the rest are badly injured. At thirty miles per hour, forty five per cent die and five per cent are injured. At twenty miles per hour, only five per cent die while thirty per cent are injured.

ACCIDENTAL CLAIMS

Among the general accident claims submitted to one British insurance company are the following:

✪ 'Wilful damage was done to the upholstery by rats'.

✪ 'I knocked over a man. He admitted it was his fault as he had been run over before.'

✪ Coming home, I drove into the wrong house and collided with a tree I have not got.'

✪ 'Cow wandered into my car. I was afterwards informed that the cow was half-witted.'

✪ 'I bumped into a lamp post obscured by pedestrians'.

NIPPY DRIVER

In 1972, a Californian motorist admitted to dangerous driving but pleaded that his attention was distracted by the shrieks of a woman passenger who was being nipped by a lobster.

TRAFFIC JAM

Congestion in Bangkok, the capital city of Thailand, is so bad that drivers are advised to carry food, water and even portable toilets when commuting. The average commuter journey takes five hours.

ROADS

The main Roman road system comprised twenty-eight great military roads, all leading to and from Rome itself.

The Roman Empire extended over eleven regions – Italy, Spain, Gaul, Britain, Illyria, Pontus, Asia Minor, Thrace, the East, Egypt and Africa. These regions, in turn, were divided into 113 provinces which were covered by 372 roads, totalling 52,694 Roman miles.

The greatest road of all was the Appian Way, which extended for 580 km (360 miles). More than 190 kilometres (120 miles) of this was paved with large stone slabs, each of which was squared and fitted exactly; the rest was paved with fitted polygons of lava. The Romans even published their own road atlas, the *Itinerarium Antonini*, compiled around AD 200.

The first man to apply sound principles to road engineering in England was 'Blind Jack' Metcalfe of Knaresborough, who had been blind since the age of six. He built 290 km (180 miles) of turnpike road in Yorkshire in the eighteenth century.

The first tarmac roads appeared in Nottinghamshire in the 1830s; the first concrete roads in Austria in the 1850s.

BICYCLES

It is estimated that more than one hundred million bicycles are sold annually around the world. World bicycle production now outpaces automobile production by three to one.

Recent Tour de France winners have all ridden bikes made of carbon fibre, a high-strength lightweight material that is also a key material in *F-14* fighter jets and Stealth aircraft.

In 1984, two students broke the US speed limit – on a tricycle. The tandem tricycle called White Lightning was the first unassisted human-powered vehicle to exceed eighty-eight kilometres (55 mph). Their reward was a honorary ticket for speeding from California's highway patrol.

A bicycle and its rider are slowed down mainly by the air resistance. At speeds higher than thirty kilometres (18 mph), it accounts for more than eighty per cent of the total force acting to slow the vehicle. That is why cyclists crouch low and wear special helmets and suits to lessen the air resistance.

In the early days of cycling, riders also discovered that wind resistance could be lessened if another rider or vehicle was in front of the cyclist.

The most famous of these was, Charles 'Mile-a-Minute' Murphy who in 1899 gained international fame by pedalling one mile at a hundred kilome-

 Hideaki Maruyama, an employee of Honda in Japan, shows off his three-wheel 'bootsmobile', which has a top speed of fifteen kilometres per hour (9mph).

tres (62.1 mph) on a bike travelling behind a train of the Long Island Rail Road on a special track built for the occasion.

The increase in the popularity of bicycling in the ninetieth century led to such a pronounced decline in church attendance that, in 1896, a Baltimore preacher was led to deliver the following condemnation from the pulpit:

'Those bladder-wheeled bicycles are diabolical devices of the demon of darkness. They are contrivances to trap the feet of the unwary and skin the nose of the innocent. They are full of guile and deceit. When you think you have broken one to ride and subdued its wild and Satanic nature, behold it bucketh you off the road and teareth a great hole in your pants. Look not on the bike when it bloweth upon its wheels for at least it bucketh like a bronco and hurteth like thunder. Who has skinned legs? Who has a bloody nose? Who has ripped breeches? They that dally along with the bicycle.'

SNOWMOBILES

Canadians own more than two million snowmobiles. Their ancestry can be traced back to the first 'Ski-Doos', produced in the winter of 1959-60 by Armand Bombardier of Valcourt, Quebec. He began work on an over-snow vehicle in 1922, at the age of fifteen, using parts from a Model-T Ford and a sleigh.

AIR FORCE ONE

Air Force One is the official title of the US President's executive aircraft when he is aboard. Originally, two *Boeing 707s* were used for this purpose, which came into service in 1962 and 1972 respectively. By 1990 even the newer aeroplane had 1,350 miles on the clock, was not large enough to carry sophisticated new communications equipment, and was too noisy for modern airports (*Concord* is five decibels quieter). A replacement had been planned since 1983 and, in the struggle to create the safest and best aircraft in the world, things got slightly out of hand.

Two *Boeing 747-200B s* were built at a cost of some $650 million ($385 million over-budget). These giant green aircraft, six stories high required a new hangar at Andrews Air Force Base ($50 million) and special service and maintenance units ($100 million). In addition, it will cost $6,000 an hour to keep the President in the air.

The new *Air Force Ones* have a range of 11,500 km (7,200 miles) and can, with mid-air refuelling, stay aloft for days in the event of a nuclear war. Each has fifty-seven antennae, anti-missile devices, 380 km (238 miles) of wire, two galleys, four computers, two photocopiers, seven lavatories, eighty-five telephones, a mini-hospital, a six-channel stereo, an eight-channel tv, a press room, and freezers that can hold enough provisions to feed its twenty-three crew members and seventy passengers for a week.

President Roosevelt became the first President to fly while in office, when he took a ninety-hour round-trip to Casablanca in 1943 for a secret rendezvous with Churchill

Harry Truman made the first internal Presidential flight. Dwight Eisenhower was the first President who was also a qualified pilot.

Air Force One took President Kennedy to Dallas and brought his body back to Washington; Lyndon Johnson took his oath of office after the assassination on board the aeroplane.

ORNITHOPTER

Two North America engineers have built and flown a radio-controlled model 'ornithopter'- an aeroplane with flapping wings like a bird – a first in aviation history. *Ornithopter 1* weighs four kilograms (9 lb) and has a wingspan of three metres (9.8 ft). It flew for just under three minutes after being hand-launched from the top of a small hill.

 A solo submarine resurfaces. The inventor is now looking for a one–man navy, a deep–sea diver who can't swim, or an agoraphobic lifeguard.

Its inventors believe that, within a few years, and with the right financial backing, they will be able to build a full-scale version that will be able to carry a person into the air.

MOLLER'S SAUCERS

Moller International, based in Davis, California, is a company which specialises in building 'flying saucers'. These craft are, in fact, two-to-four-person vertical take-off and landing (VTOL) aircraft which their inventor, Paul Moller, believes will function in the future as affordable high-speed commuter aircraft.

The prototype, *M200X* has eight small rotary engines set in a circle round the edge of the craft; the pilot sits in the centre inside a clear bubble-cockpit.

AIRSHIPS

The smallest airship in the world is an eighteen-metre (60 ft) craft built by students at Southampton University. Its transparent nylon plastic envelope is filled with 165 cubic metres (5,800 cu ft) of helium and is propelled forward by a cyclist sitting in an aluminium cage below.

FANTASTIC PHENOMENA!

COINCIDENCE

In 1891, a novel called, *The Wreck of the Titan* by American author Morgan Robertson was published. Morgan claimed to write his novels whilst in a trance-like state.

The book describes the tragic maiden voyage of the largest luxury liner ever built, the 'unsinkable' *Titan*. Seventy-five thousand tons of dead-weight, she had three propellers and could travel at a top speed of twenty-five knots, carrying 2-3,000 passengers. One foggy night in April, the *Titan* crashed into an iceberg and sank. There were only twenty-four lifeboats on board and many people lost their lives.

This fictional plot bears an uncanny resemblance to the real-life *Titanic* disaster. Built in 1904, the *Titanic* was the largest craft afloat of her time and had the same reputation for invulnerability. She also weighed 75,000 tons, had three screws and a top speed of twenty-five knots. On her maiden voyage in

1912, the *Titanic* sunk after hitting an iceberg in thick fog on the night of April 15. There were 2,207 passengers on board but only twenty lifeboats. As a result, 1,500 people died.

THIRTEEN

An Eton schoolboy named Baxter, proved mathematically that the thirteenth day of the month is more likely to fall on Friday than on any other day, in a scientific paper published when he was thirteen.

Friday is traditionally regarded as an unlucky day, because of Christ's crucifixion and the belief that it was on a Friday that Adam and Eve ate from the Tree of Knowledge.

The thirteenth *Apollo* mission, launched at 1313 hours from pad thirty-nine (13 x 3) had to be aborted on the thirteenth of April 1970.

The morbid fear of the number thirteen is called, 'Triskaidekaphobia' (*triskaideka* is Greek for thirteen).

Composer, Arnold Schoenberg was born on 13 September 1874. Being a triskaidekaphobic, he believed that he would die in his seventy-sixth year (7+6 =13). Not only did this prove true, but he also died on Friday 13 July 1951 at thirteen minutes to midnight.

The superstition about the ill-fated consequences of dining with thirteen people at the table (Jesus was the thirteenth at the table) is of very ancient origin. It is believed that the first person to rise from the dinner table will die before the year is out. The only solution to the dilemma is for guests to leap from their seats at exactly the same moment. Amongst those who shared this superstition was Napoleon, the billionaire John Paul Getty, and US Presidents Herbert Hoover and Franklin D. Roosevelt. In Paris, a professional guest – a 'Quatorzieme' – can be hired at short notice.

Margaret Thatcher was born on 13 October and married on 13 December.

MYSTERIOUS IMPRINT

At six o'clock in the morning of the 9 March 1981, a forty-four year-old West Indian named Les died from cancer of the pancreas in a hospice in Thornton, Lancashire.

By the time Nurse Patricia Oliver came on duty, the body had been taken away by the undertakers, wrapped in the hospital bedsheet. She followed the normal practice of clearing away the pyjamas which had been removed from the patient's body, and washed the synthetic protective mattress cover.

On this occasion everything proved far from normal. After fruitlessly trying to remove what appeared to be a stain on the mattress cover, the nurse realised with a shock what it was – a ghostly image of a naked body from head to foot, with hand, palm upwards and face twisted downwards.

Other staff-members were equally astonished. To this day there is no explanation for this imprinting, particularly when you consider that the patient was wearing pyjamas, his head was resting on a pillow and there was a sheet between him and the mattress cover.

UFOS

It has now been confirmed, by investigative journalist Howard Blum, that the US government is engaged in 'an ongoing covert search for extraterrestrial life'. A UFO Working Group meets regularly in the Tank, the most secure conference room in the Pentagon.

Officially, the government's interest in UFOs ended in 1969 with Project Blue Book, code name for an Air Force study of 12,618 alleged UFO sightings over a twenty-two-year period.

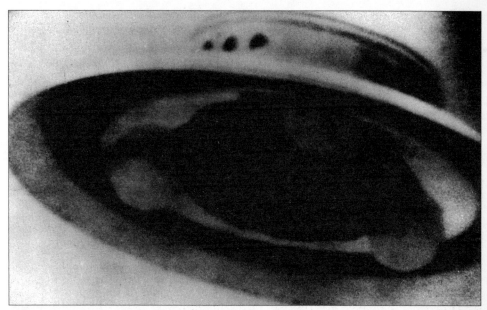

 An alleged photo of a UFO, shot over California in 1952. Real or fake, its now confirmed that the phenomenon is being officially studied by the US government.

 Despite the best efforts of disciples of transcendental meditation guru Mahareshi Mahesh Yogi, the force of gravity still works, so these yogic flyers land with a bump.

Dr John Mack is a Harvard psychiatrist who has helped fifty patients overcome the traumas caused, they believe, by the fact that they have been abducted by aliens.

Dr Mack, who has organised a conference for abductees, says: 'I don't have an explanation. But I know they've undergone a powerful sense of being intruded upon.'

His colleague, historian David Jacobs, is the author of *Secret Life: Firsthand Accounts of UFO Abductions*. He also teaches a university course 'UFOs in US Society'. He believes that aliens are engaged in 'a programme of systematic exploitation' of the human species.

Philip Mantle, a printer from Batley, West Yorkshire, lectures on UFOs at Leeds University and builds models of alien creatures based on abductee reports.

There is a striking similarity between all the accounts, producing iden-tikit descriptions of two main types of creature:

The first are small ugly beings, three to five feet tall, with large pear-shaped heads, big round eyes and slit noses and mouths. They have grey, wrinkled skin are usually hairless and often wear green uniforms. They often stun their subject with a beam of light and conduct medical experiments on them.

The second type are thin, more than six feet tall, have long blond hair, pale skins, blue or pink cat-like eyes and wear silver or grey suits. They appear kindly and god-like and are attempting to convey messages about their planet.

Philip Mantle is interested in the whole phenomena but does not believe that UFOs are of extraterrestrial origin. He explains the sightings as either man-made objects, natural phenomena or parapsychological events – in the same category as visions of angels or chariots of fire, fairies or ghosts.

There appears to have been a decline in sightings of UFOs since the end of the Cold War.

BALL LIGHTNING

Balls of lightning, typically twenty-five centimetres (10 in) in diameter and glowing a pale red or orange colour, remain a widely reported but little understood natural phenomena.

They literally appear out of the blue, often with a halo surrounding them, sometimes emitting sparks and a sulphurous smell, and last anything up to a minute before disappearing again.

Various attempts have been made to recreate ball lightning in the laboratory with limited success. Many scientists now concede its reality but find it incomprehensible.

A Professor of Electronics from Kent University was on an Eastern Airlines flight from New York to Washington when, at five minutes past midnight, a blue-white glowing sphere came out of the pilot's cabin and travelled down the aircraft's aisle about seventy-five centimetres (2½ ft) above the floor.

In 1981, an amateur astronomer from Te Ngaere in New Zealand, rushed into her house carrying some wet steel tools to escape a thunderstorm when, she recalls:

'I looked up as the whole house shook and then looked down and saw a flow of light come in under the door. It settled in a blob [from which] arms flowed out like runs of oil among the tools There was no sound or smell. The arms finally went back into the blob which disappeared again suddenly out under the door.'

The whole episode lasted about fifteen seconds. This case was investigated by two physicists who concluded it was some kind of magnetic phenomena.

A correspondent of the magazine, *New Scientist* reported that his mother and aunt had told him, when he was very young, that they'd seen a ball of light appear in the air, strike a tram pole and blow the fuses on it.

Another friend, while sheltering from a storm, had seen such a ball appear, roll down the road and then explode, sending a manhole cover flying through the air.

More evidence for the existence of ball lightning comes from the oil industry. In 1976 two employees of the Amoco Oil Research Department described eight incidents where ball lightning was reported responsible for explosions of petrol trucks and tankers. Eyewitnesses describe 'a ball of light' entering the truck's petrol tank before the explosion.

POWER-SURGE HOUSE

Scientists remain baffled about the exact cause of the energy beam that runs through a small, terraced cottage in Somerton, Somerset, causing power-surges of more than 12,000 volts.

Its owner, Frank Pattemore, has had to replace thousands of fuses and hundreds of light bulbs. The surges have blown kettle elements and wrecked five tv sets. Lamp shades have burst into flames and meals have been ruined in the cooker so often, Frank and his son rely on relatives for hot food.

The local electricity board has rewired the house three times and now supplies all Frank's light bulbs. But they can find no explanation for the surges.

The cottage is located near a British Telecom radio station and is a few miles from the Royal Naval Air Station at Yeovilton. But the Ministry of Defence denies that they operate any equipment that could cause the problem.

HAIRY HANDS

The road between Two Bridges and Postbridge runs through the very heart of Dartmoor. It is haunted by a pair of disembodied hairy hands – so local legend has it.

A certain Dr Ernest Helby, a prison doctor, was travelling this road on his motorbike in 1921, with two children in the side-car. Suddenly he told them to jump out. The motorbike swerved violently off the road and Dr Helby died in the crash. The children survived and claimed they had seen hairy hands on the handlebars.

Two months later, a young army officer was flung from his motorbike on the same stretch of road. he told reporters that something drove him off the road. 'A pair of hands closed over mine...large muscular hairy hands.' There have been plenty of more recent incidents to keep the story alive.

There are true believers, and those who put it down to drinking too much cider. Is it just a folk tale or could it be that the hands are the ghostly remains of an Italian who worked in a local gunpowder factory? One night, so the story goes, he came into some money and went out with friends to celebrate. When drunk, he forgot about his hobnail boots, which created a spark and blew him into the hereafter.

Psi, from which the word, 'psychic' is derived, comes from the twenty-third letter of the Greek alphabet, the symbol of the unknown.

YOGIC FLYING

Followers of the Indian guru, Maharishi Mahesh Yogi believe that transcendental meditation can bring about world peace. They practice 'yogic flying'. This involves bouncing up and down on mattresses with your legs crossed. Experts can hop over six-inch hurdles. None has yet achieved the second stage but several talk hopefully of reach it : hovering.

The yogic flyers believe their actions have helped ease industrial strife, reduce crime and promote general well being. Flyers, they believe, tap into the 'unified field', the meeting-point of all natural and cosmic energies, which then transmits goodness to others.

MAGNETIC ROADWAY

Croy Brae in Strathclyde, Scotland is one of the most disorientating places on earth.

If you approach the *brae* (hill) from the north it looks as if road slopes downwards; in fact, it runs uphill. The reverse is the case if you approach from the south. You appear to be heading up hill but are actually going down.

The cause of this phenomena is still unclear but it appears to be a combination of the unusual lie of the land and a variation in the earth's magnetic field, which may interfere with our sense of balance and orientation.

There are similar places in other parts of the world: on a road into Jerusalem near the village of Djabal Moukaber; two places in Canada, one near Vancouver and another called Moncton Hill in New Brunswick; and at Mystery Hill in North Carolina.

GRIMSBY GHOSTBUSTERS

There is a real 'Ghostbusters' team – in Grimsby. It consists of, Robin Furman, a psychologist and hypnotherapist, his son Andrew, Rodney Mitchell and Janice Paterson.

Andrew is in charge of the Ghostmobile, an old Austin Princess that once belonged to the Mayor of Cleethorpes. Rodney, a computer consultant, invented the 'Roboghost' which sniffles out vibrations, and other spectral phenomena. The fifth member of the team is a huge Newfoundland dog named Ben.

SLIME GHOST

A slime ghost appears to be inhabiting a semi-detached council house on the outskirts of Leicester, the home of the Boulter family.

According to one eyewitness reporter, the house 'resembles a monsoon casualty'. Everything is covered with plastic sheeting as sticky deposits of slime appear all over the house – in the fridge, on beds and chairs, inside wardrobes and drawers. A glob of slime even landed in the goldfish tank, killing the fish.

Visitor's handbags have filled with slime, the video has gone gooey, the phone has broken and plugs and fires have been put out of action by this strange substance.

At present, there is no rational explanation for this phenomenon.

CRYSTAL SKULLS

Mystery still surrounds the origin of two strange life-sized crystal skulls, one which is in the collection of the Museum of Mankind in London, the other, more famous one, which is in a private collection in Canada.

The latter, known as the 'Mitchell-Hedges Skull' was supposedly discovered under an altar in the ruins of the Mayan city of Lubaantun in Belize (formerly British Honduras) in Central America. It appears to have been made from a form of rock crystal found in California.

Sceptics believe it was planted there by Fredric Mitchell-Hedges, the British archaeologist and explorer, so that his adopted daughter, Anna would find it on her birthday.

Others claim that Mitchell-Hedges bought the skull from a British owner in the 1940s and made up the story of its discovery.

Whatever the truth, the skull is an extraordinary work in its own right – beautifully finished, eerie in its perfection and carved in such a way that light is concentrated in the eye sockets.

An art restorer who studied it for many years reported many strange phenomena. The skull filled with mist, produced a strange perfume and tinkling sounds, changed colour, and was once surrounded by an aura.

The other skull was supposedly brought from Mexico by a Spanish official and sold to an English collector, from where it passed through many hands before reaching the museum.

It is officially dated from the Aztec period (14-1500 AD) but other experts are not so sure, claiming its origin is anything but Aztec.

Both skulls are made from a form of gem-like quartz found almost exclusively in Brazil, Calveras County in California and in Madagascar. This mineral is also used to make the crystal balls favoured by fortune tellers.

SPONTANEOUS HUMAN COMBUSTION

Reports of spontaneous human combustion (SHC) have a long history but there is still controversy as to whether any of them are true. There is still no fully accepted explanation as to how SHC might occur .

SHC is an internal burning of the body which rapidly reduces all except the head and feet to a heap of ashes, often leaving objects in the near vicinity unscorched. An intense level of heat would be needed to achieve this; in crematoriums, temperatures of 900 °C (1,650 °F) are needed to burn a body and, even then, it takes a couple of hours.

In Scotland in 1904, a certain Mrs Cochrane, a widow of Falkirk, was found 'burned beyond recognition' in a chair stuffed with pillows, which were not even scorched. There was no fire in the grate.

British researcher, Tony McMunn, who has devoted ten years to studying the subject, claims ninety-eight per cent of the cases he has examined can be explained away, leaving a troublesome two per cent which appear to support the existence of SHC.

One of these cases concerns a non-drinking, non-smoking Birmingham student who appears to have suddenly burst into flames in his bed. The photographic evidence shows that the sheets displayed only slight scorch marks. There was no obvious ignition source.

Author, Jenny Randle worked for seven years with co-author Peter Hough on their book *Spontaneous Human Combustion*. She estimates that between ten and one hundred people burst into flames in Britain every year.

She believes that freak combinations of gases and foods inside the body could be responsible for the phenomena. 'A combination of hydrocarbons from eating too many eggs, and medicine to control bowel movements which consists of liquid paraffin could, according to some scientists, be a 'flammable combination.'

Larry E. Arnold, from Harrisburg, Pennsylvania records the story of a Toronto woman who woke up to find she had second and third-degree burns on her abdomen and thighs; there were no burn marks on her night-gown or sheets. She had to undergo six months of skin grafts to repair the wounds.

BUBBLES

According to mathematics professor, Anthony Tromba: 'The soap bubble is one of the simple profundities of nature. That is why soap films have been studied since the eighteenth century and, believe it or not, have become one of the most important areas of research in modern mathematics.'

The colours that swirl around the surface of bubbles are caused by interference of light waves. Some are reflected from the outside surface and some from the inside. The colours change as the soap film gets thinner from evaporation. The skin of a bubble is only a few millionths of an inch thick.

The most important researcher in the history of bubbles was Joseph A.F. Plateau,

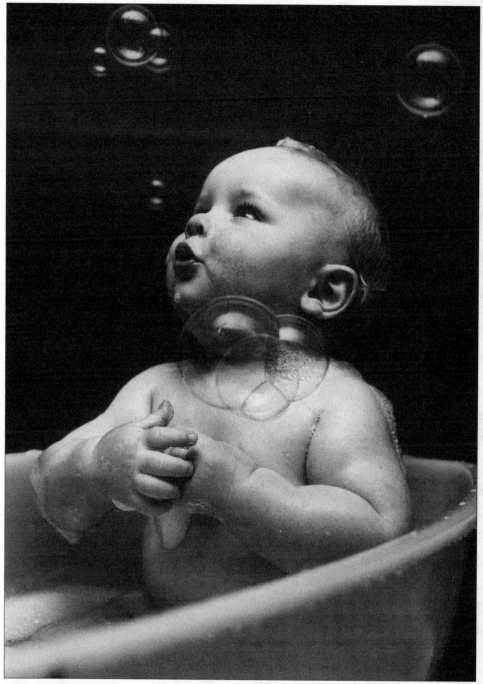

 A young researcher experimenting with what one scientist has called 'one of the simple profundities of nature' – soap bubbles.

a Belgian physicist. He was the man who discovered that bubbles can only connect in one of two angles – either 109 or 120 degrees. His two-volume work, the distillation of a lifetime's research, is still widely regarded as the standard work on the subject.

He accomplished this work despite the fact that, for much of his life, he was blind. At the age of twenty-eight, he stared at the sun for several minutes to investigate an idea he had about optics. As a result, he suffered a gradual loss of vision which became total fourteen years later.

Dr Aristid Grosse, an American physicist, is probably the leading expert on bizarre bubbles and funny foams. He was once the owner of the world's oldest bubble and his office is home to a huge collection of ageing bubbles (at various stages of decay) preserved in glass bell jars.

One way of making unusual bubbles is to slice up horse chestnuts ('conkers') and soak them in a little water. The slightly yellow liquid that results contains a substance called 'saponine', which can be used to blow bubbles up to three or four inches in diameter. The skin of these is gel-like; when burst, they collapse like a wrinkled bag.

The elder statesman, spiritual grandfather and wizard of modern bubble-blowing is the unlikely named Eiffel Plasterer, a retired high school physics teacher, now in his eighties, who lives on a farm in Indiana. He has performed his show, the 'Bubble Concerto' more than 1,400 times in the last fifty years. He can build 1.2 m (4 ft) bubble chains, multi-coloured bubble castles and hydrogen bubbles that explode in mid-air into puffs of flame. He can put bubbles inside bubbles, ships inside bubbles, even people inside bubbles.

He believes: 'Life is not a bubble, but like blowing a bubble. We are always expanding our hopes, dreams and aspirations.'

NUMBERS

The chances of getting a complete suit dealt to you at bridge is 158,753,389,999 to one. This actually happened to Bill McNall at the Carlton Club in Gateshead in March 1992. He dealt himself a hand consisting of all thirteen hearts.

584834 is the only number (other than nought or one) equal to the sum of the sixth powers of its digits.

What is so special about the number 8549176320?. The digits come in alphabetical order.

BIRTHDAY PROBLEM

How many people do you need in a group before you find two of them with the same birthday ? The answer – surprisingly – is twenty-three. Why should this be ?

In a small group of people, there is a one-in-nine chance (11.7%) of at least two identical birthdays. By the time you have reached twenty people, the odds have reached 41.1%

As the size of the group rises arithmetically, the number of two-person combinations rises geometrically. In a group of twenty-three there are 253 possible combinations.

In his book, *Lady Luck*, Warren Weaver tells the story of how, during World War II, he was explaining this problem at a dinner-party where a number of high-ranking military officers were present.

He recounts: 'Noticing that there were exactly twenty-two at the table, someone proposed we run a test. We got all the way around the table without a duplicate birthday. At which point a waitress remarked, "Excuse me. But I am the twenty-third person in the room and my birthday is May 17, just like the General's over there."'.

IRREPRODUCIBLE RESULTS

The Journal of Irreproducible Results has been described as a kind of *Mad* magazine of the science world, full of straight-faced scientific papers about crazy things.

One of its most famous articles – *National Geographic; The Doomsday Machine* by George H. Kaub – predicted that if everyone keeps stacking *National Geographics* in garages and attics instead of throwing them away, the magazines' weight will sink the continents to a depth of thirty metres (100 ft) some time soon and we will all be inundated by the oceans.

At the time it was written, more than 6.8 million issues of the magazine, each weighing 0.9 kg (2 lb), were sent to subscribers, monthly. The article claims that not one has been thrown away since publication began 141 years ago.

The author blames the rise in earthquake activity in California on a rise in population growth and the subsequent increase in *National Geographic* subscriptions.

Another article, called *Pickles Humbug* reported the striking discovery that pickles cause cancer, communism, air crashes , car crashes and crime waves.

It pointed out that 99.9% of cancer victims have eaten pickles some time in their lives as have a hundred per cent of all soldiers, 96.8 % of Communist sympathizers and 99.7% of those involved in car and air crashes.

Moreover, one hundred per cent of those people who ate pickles in 1839 are now dead; rats, force-fed twenty pounds of pickles a day for a month, end up with bulging abdomens and loss of appetite.

Another article came up with a novel solution to protect the Grand Canyon, which is being destroyed through a combination of air pollution and soil erosion. The answer, according to Earle Spamer of the Academy of Natural Sciences in Philadelphia, is to fill the canyon with about four billion cubic metres

(1 cu mile) of polystyrene packaging chips, at a cost of five billion dollars.

If somebody worked out a permanent way to save the canyon and the chips needed to be removed, they could be puffed away using a number of large leaf-blowers. The author suggests that if they happen to engulf Las Vegas, that would be an added benefit.

MR ELECTRICITY

In 1987, after thirteen years teaching classes in geology, biology, chemistry, archaeology and physics at the Memphis Museum, Tennessee , Robert Krampf decided to leave and tour the country with a travelling high-voltage electricity show. In the first five years, he has travelled 25,000 miles and performed before half a million students.

Robert Krampf uses a one million-volt Tesla coil in his shows, which converts regular household *direct* current (DC) into very special high-frequency *alternating* current (AC).

The electricity in the wires of your home move back and forth in the wires fifty times per second; this special AC current alternates at a rate of 280,000 times per second. This gives the electricity some unusual properties: it flows round objects rather than through them.

That explain why it is possible for him to sit in a metal cage (called the Faraday cage) while a million volts play around him. Due to what is called the 'skin effect', the electricity stays on the outside without harming the person inside. This demonstration also explains why a car is safe during a lightning storm. It has nothing to do with the rubber tyres, as most people think. It is because the lightning flows round the car as it does the cage.

The Tesla coil can produce a lightning-like spark up to 1.5 m (4½ ft) long and it can light a fluorescent bulb held in the hand 1.2 m (4 ft) away.

ROBOTS

The word, 'robot' was coined by the Czech playwright, Karel Capek in his play R.U.R in 1921. It was derived from the word *robotit*, which is Czech for 'to drudge'.

A team of researchers in the laboratory of robotics at the University of Amiens in France, have built a robot that moves like an earthworm. It is designed to be used for the inspection and maintenance of the tubular pipework in nuclear power plants and in the complex structures of spacecraft.

Conventional robots, which have tracks or wheels, are ideal for flat surfaces but are no use where there are random obstacles or unpredictable changes in gradient.

These robot worms are made up of autonomous segments of different lengths, each of which can curve in three directions, which move by waves of contractions and elongation passing along the whole length of it. Separate mechanical limbs down each side help the robot to grip on a slippery surface.

At Portsmouth Polytechnic in England, a team of researchers have developed a six-legged robot, inspired by the cockroach. Each of its legs can move independently; they have small electrical microprocessors attached to a central one which acts as the robot's brain. The first practical application was intended for bomb disposal work. The leader of the team, Arthur Collie, also dreams of using these kind of robots as means of transport in countries like Africa.

Dr Rodney Brooks and his team at the Massachusetts Institute of Technology also models his robots on insects. He imagines small and robust mechanical bugs that could explore distant planets or scurry round your house cleaning up dust.

He suggests: 'A squadron of gnat robots could even mow the lawn, with each one crawling up a blade of grass and then cutting it off – the perfect manicure.'

Their planetary explorer robot is called Atilla. It weighs 1.5 kg (3.5 lb) and is fitted with eleven microchips, twenty-four activators and 150 sensors – all at a unit cost of twelve thousand pounds.

This modest cost means that a lot of them can be used and built and also quickly adapted to incorporate new ideas and technology.

The robots are designed to be like babies: they explore and learn from their experience, building up data, layer upon layer, developing behaviour that, if not intelligent, may be useful.

A rancher from Tennessee named Charles D. McVean has invested more than two million dollars in developing a radio-controlled robot jockey. Named 'Super-Jock', it weighs ten kilograms (22 lb), is made of glass fibre and metal, can handle the reins, shout, 'giddap' and urge its horse onwards by wielding a whip attached to its own bottom. It is small enough to race indoors on Hackney ponies, a spirited breed that are less than half the size of a racehorse and only one-tenth of the price.

McVean actually set out to develop a robot cowboy to patrol his spread of ten thousand acres. He has created what he hopes will be, a major sport of the future.

'Manny' is the name of a robot-mannequin developed at a cost of two million dollars by the Battelle Laboratories in Richland, Washington for the US Army.

It resembles the human body in size, limb and trunk geometry. It can simulate complex body movements. It poses, breathes, changes its skin and body temperatures and sweats. It has about forty articulated joints, driven by hydraulic pumps, that allow it to walk, bend, squat and crawl.

Manny is used, mainly to test the effectiveness of the clothing used to protect soldiers from chemical and biological weapons, from extreme temperatures and from hostile environments.

The world's first robot sheep-shearer was developed in Australia in the early 1980s. According to its inventors, it can follow the contours of a struggling sheep and instantly adjust the cutters to keep them above the skin.

In 1985 a robot-arm danced the central role in a modern ballet, entitled *Invisible Cities*, at Stanford University in California. The robot, which was anchored to a table top, was programmed to move in time to a composition by Chopin. It

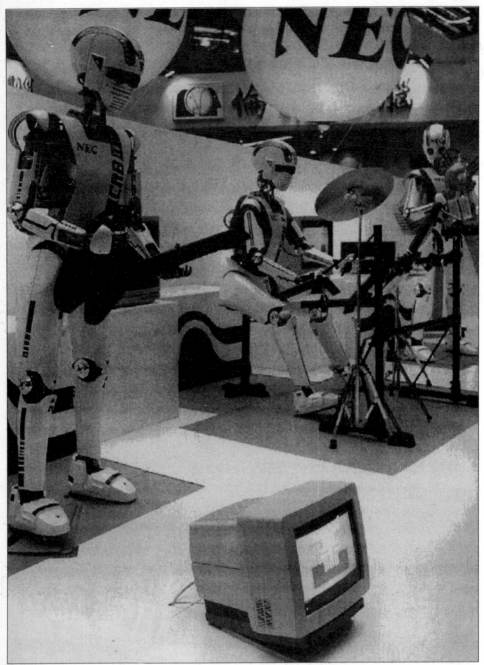

 A robot band, built by NEC Taiwan Ltd, play the Carpenters' song 'Top of the World' at the Taipei World Trade Centre in December 1990. They cost more than $700,000 and are capable of 64 movements each.

performed a lively solo piece and also partnered human dancer, Katie Nelson. Because she could have been injured by the force of the arm, which weighed fifty-four kilograms (120 lb), a panic button was attached to the 'arm', in case anything went wrong.

The event was highly successful and was filmed in order to show disabled people the grace and precision that is now possible with a mechanical aid.

Ichiro Kato, a professor at Waseda University in Japan, spent three years with fifty of his students, building an organ-playing robot for an Expo at Tsukuba.

The robot, called 'Wabot-2', had limbs which could move through twenty-five different axes, and a camera eye that could scan a sheet of music in fifteen seconds.

MASSES

The mass of a virus is to the mass of an average man as the mass of an average man is to the mass of the Earth

The mass of an electron is to a water melon as a water melon is to the sun.

It is estimated that there are four hundred million billion molecules in a cubic inch of air.

METABOLISM

Santoro Sanctorius, founder of the science of metabolism, spent much of his time, over a thirty year period, sitting on a weighing device to calculate variations in his body-weight before and after eating, drinking, sleeping, exercise and so on. He carefully weighed all the food and drink he ingested as well as the excreta that he passed and was able to make exact measurements of the weight he lost due to water evaporation.

PHOSPHOROUS

Phosphorous, a word derived from the Greek, meaning' light-bearing', was first isolated from human urine by a Hamburg alchemist in 1670. An entrepreneur bought the secret of the process and toured Europe exhibiting this new substance. A vogue developed for the medical use of phosphorous, which was claimed to cure all ills.

Its most practical use though was for matches. Prototypes produced in 1780 featured a wax paper with a phosphorous tip encased in a glass tube. Breaking the tube exposed the phosphorous to air, causing it to ignite.

Friction matches appeared in 1826. They were known as 'lucifers' and were first produced by John Walker, an English chemist. Their manufacture led to workers developing an industrial disease called 'phossy-jaw' in which chronic phosphorous poisoning caused decay of teeth, gums and jawbones.

JUNK

Space has become a vast junkyard. An estimated 3,000 tonnes of junk now orbit the earth, the majority of which consists of fragments less than one centimetre (⅓in) in size.

A particle one millimetre (⅟₃₀ in) in diameter, travelling at sixteen kilometres per hour (10 mph), hits an object with the force of a seven kilogram (16 lb) bowling ball. One pound of space junk, travelling at a modest 160 km per hour (100 mph), hits a craft with the force of a fifty tonne locomotive moving at the same speed.

At present, US Space Command can track only fragments larger than 10 cm (4 in) – a mere 7,059 objects out of the estimated total of 3.5 million.

The greatest number of tracked objects is in low-earth orbit (LEO). Here, space crews operating outside their spacecraft are threatened by super-fast particles that could penetrate their space suits. A metal chip 0.5 mm ($\frac{1}{100}$ inch) wide and travelling at ten kilometres per second (6 miles/sec) could easily kill an astronaut. A particle a few centimetres in diameter could destroy part of a space station.

Accidental and deliberate explosions have created forty-nine per cent of the debris in space. Between 1973 and 1981, seven US *Delta* rockets exploded in orbit. Between 1964 and 1986, the deliberate destruction of thirty-four satellites for security reasons generated 20,984 fragments. All but three of these were Soviet.

In 1986, an *Ariane* rocket blew up in the worst single break-up in history. The explosion created 465 objects and a further 23,000 smaller particles which spread out around the earth, eventually forming a shell.

When NASA's *Skylab* fell into the Indian Ocean in 1979, its eighty-tonne mass disintegrated, scattering a trail 1,000 km (620 miles) long in five hundred major fragments, some travelling at supersonic speed.

In 1982, part of an old Soviet rocket missed the space shuttle *Columbia* by only twelve kilometres (7 miles). In 1983, a speck of paint travelling at 3-6 km/sec (2-4 miles/sec) created a cavity three millimetres ($\frac{1}{8}$ inch) in diameter in *Challenger's* windscreen. Ground crew had to replace the windscreen before the shuttle could be re-launched. Shielding satellites against particles larger than one centimetre ($\frac{1}{3}$ in) would make them too heavy to launch.

The quantity of space debris is increasing and could leave us earthbound within thirty years. Some scientists believe that so much debris will accumulate that random collisions will set off an avalanche of secondary collisions in a runaway cascade. The resulting belt of small debris could make space flight impossible for several centuries.

TINTIN'S ROCKET

A replica of the moon rocket designed by Professor Calculus in the Tintin books *Destination Moon* and *Explorers of the Moon*, was launched at the Kourou space centre in French Guiana on 21 July 1989 in tribute to the twentieth anniversary of the first Moon landing.

The rocket, known as *RG1* after the initials of Hergé's real name, Remy George, is made of epoxy, weighs eleven kilograms (24 lb) and stands 157 cm (5 ft) tall. It can reach an altitude of 2,000 metres (1.2 miles) in twenty-five seconds.

The rocket is powered by a special engine called 'Bambi', which uses gunpowder as a fuel. This is necessary because considerable force is required to overcome the drag caused by the rocket's vast tail fins, which are an aerodynamic nightmare.

METEORITE MAN

Robert Haag is the only full-time meteorite-hunter and dealer in the world, supplying museums, planetariums, universities and private collectors.

Fascinated by them since he was a child, Haag believes that around five hundred meteorites land on the Earth every year (most burn up in the atmosphere) but only five or six of these are spotted. That means there are million of meteorites just lying around waiting to be found.

In less than fifteen years, he has built up the world's largest private collection of meteorites and become a millionaire in the process.

He has roamed the world searching for rare examples for his collection and his been involved in many Indiana-Jones style adventures.

In Argentina he was arrested after purchasing for $40,000, the world's third- largest meteorite – a thirty-seven tonne mass of iron and stone, the size of a small car. When he attempted to export it he was arrested for theft, although charges were later dropped.

He was also in dispute with the Western Australian government after he acquired a rare piece of moon rock, found by Aborigines working for him. It is the only piece of moon rock now in private hands and is worth an estimated ten million dollars.

ANIMALS IN SPACE

A great many more insects and animals than human beings have gone into space.

The first fish in space were a group of South American guppies that spent forty-eight days in a zero-gravity aquarium on board the Russian *Salyut 5* space station in 1976.

There was a large selection of mice and flies on the *Cosmos 936* flight in September 1977.

A five-year programme at two New Jersey schools to put ants into space ended on a sad note. After their June 1987 voyage on board the *Challenger* space shuttle an autopsy was carried out. They discovered the ants had died of dehydration, a month before take-off, in their sealed container. When they came back dead, it was assumed they died in earth orbit.

The *Endeavour* space shuttle mission, launched on 12 September 1992, was unusual in two respects. It was the first to have a husband and wife team on board. Secondly it had a menagerie which included four South African Clawed frogs, two Japanese carp, 180 Oriental hornets, 7,600 fruit flies and thirty fertilized chicken eggs.

A two-foot tall stuffed version of a cartoon dog named Digswell, the mascot of America's Young Astronauts Council, was carried into space aboard a Russian *Soyuz* rocket capsule on 16 November 1992. The rocket was emblazoned with the worlds 'The World Welcomes Digswell'. The spacecraft splashed down off Seattle on America's West Coast and was recovered by the Russian warship, *Marshal Krilov.*

The Russian-US space mission, timed to mark the 500th anniversary of Columbus's discovery of the New World, was privately funded by a Russian businessman as a gesture to try and cement trade links with the US and encourage youth interest in space.

SPACE FOOD

Bread dries out in space which is why space shuttle missions carry tortillas instead.

Early spaceflight food came out of a tube because it was believed humans wouldn't be able to swallow in space. Now astronauts use knives and forks and eat as we do.

However, there is limited space for cooking and refrigeration. Many foods are dehydrated (just add water); others are thermo-stabilised, that is they are pre-cooked and sealed ready to be warmed up in a small oven.

People eat less in space but need the same number of calories. Tex-Mex food is popular to counteract blandness and stimulate the appetite.

Foods that coalesce, like yoghurts, are important in a weightless environment; it means your spoon might float off but your food will stay on it.

Part of the fun for astronauts is that they're allowed to play with their food.

When French astronaut, Colonel Jean-Loup Chrétien joined Soviet cosmonauts on a joint mission in 1982, he was well supplied. A series of special space gourmet meals was prepared for him including jugged hare, crab soup and lobster pilaf with sauce á l'Armoricaine. This heavy food was designed to test the reactions of the body's cardiovascular systems during the flight.

Space shuttle menus currently feature more than seventy different food items and twenty different drinks.

PLANETS

The surface of Venus has a temperature of 480 °C (876° F), an atmosphere composed of carbon dioxide which is ninety times denser than Earth's, and sulphuric acid rain.

Two-thirds of its landscape consists of rolling plain; much of the rest is lowland, with only eight per cent being highlands, comparable to Earth's continents.

The planet is peppered with tens of thousands of volcanoes and more than eighty per cent of the planet is covered with exceptionally runny lava. The largest volcano, Maat Mons is eight kilometres high (5 miles).

It is also studded with meteorite craters, despite the fact that the planet's thick atmosphere provides a shield against space debris. Some 900 craters have been identified to date, the largest being Cleopatra, which is one hundred kilometres (62 miles) across.

The Moon spin round in just over twenty-seven days; a 'day' there is almost as long as two Earth weeks, with a 'night' of the same length.

Jupiter's Great Red Spot is a tremendous atmospheric storm that rotates

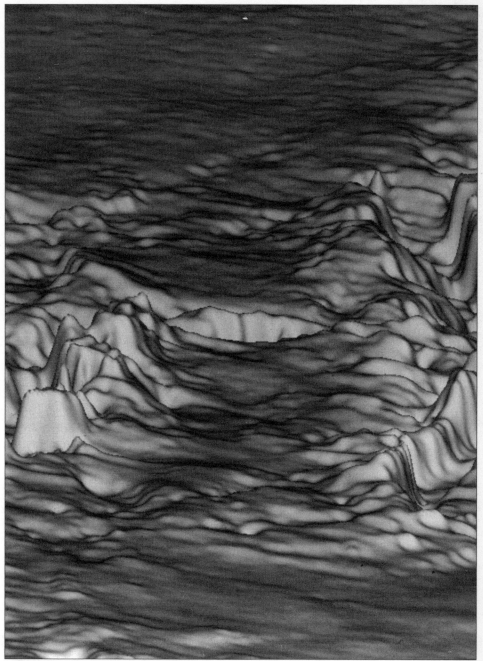

 Data obtained from the US *Magellan* spacecraft was used to generate this perspective view of the topography of two valleys on the surface of Venus.

counter-clockwise with one revolution every six days. The Spot is the coldest place on the planet and covers an area of about 48,000 km (30,000 miles) long and 11,250 km (7,000 miles) wide. In other words, about three times the surface area of the Earth. It is believed the Spot hangs about twenty-four kilometres (15 miles) above the surrounding clouds.

Neptune has a Great Dark Spot in its atmosphere. First detected by the spacecraft, *Voyager 2* in the winter of 1988-9, it is also a massive storm which appears to churn in an anti-clockwise direction, taking eighteen hours to complete a rotation. This is slightly faster than the rotation of the planet itself, which completes one rotation in sixteen hours and seven minutes. As a result, the Spot is moving westward at a speed of 1,000 km per hour (600 mph).

The surface of the sun is at a temperature of around 6,000 °C (11,000 °F); near its core it's estimated to be nearer fourteen million °C (25 million °F).

Huge nuclear reactions power the sun, changing hydrogen into helium. Energy and mass are lost in the process and the Sun is actually losing four million tonnes of its mass every second.

On Mercury. there are craters named after composers, Beethoven and Chopin, the poet Coleridge, architect Sir Christopher Wren and writer Mark Twain; valleys named after radar installations (Arecibo and Goldstone), plains named after the name of Mercury in different Earth-languages (such as *Suisei*, the name of the planet in Japanese); ridges named after famous ships (*Discovery, Endeavour*) and after astronomers whose work has been closely associated with the planet (Antoniadi).

Mercury has daytime surface temperatures of as high as 430 °C (800 °F). In November 1992 scientists reported that a new radar study of this hellish planet had found ice at its poles. How is this possible ?

It appears that, although the poles are bathed in scorching sunlight, the light hits at a shallow angle and some craters are thus permanently in shadow and the temperature there is below zero. Thus any ice that formed billions of years ago during the planet's creation, when water boiled on the planet's surface and then condensed as frost, would still be there.

The largest volcano in our solar system is Olympus Mons, which has a base 600 km (370 miles) in diameter. It is three times the height of Everest.

Also on Mars is a complicated network of canyons known as the 'Valles Marineris', which stretches for 4,000 km (2,400 miles). Individual canyons within the system are 200 km (120 miles) wide and seven kilometres (4 miles) deep.

By contrast, Arizona's Grand Canyon is only 450 km (280 miles) long, two kilometres (1¼ miles*) deep and thirty kilometres (18 miles) wide at most.

The South Pole of Mars is capped with carbon dioxide ice. Carbon dioxide accounts for about ninety-five per cent of the thin, Martian atmosphere; about twenty per cent of it freezes at the south pole every winter.

SUPERNOVA

A supernova is the name for the collapse and explosion of a massive star. During the first ten seconds of its creation, the core of the star implodes to form a neutron star. As much energy is radiated from its thirty-two kilometre (20 mile) – wide central region as from all the other stars and galaxies in the rest of the visible universe combined.

Another way of expressing it is that the energy released in that ten-second burst is one hundred times more than the sun will radiate in its entire ten billion-year lifetime.

In human history there have been very few supernovas recorded. One flared up in our galaxy in 1604, just before the invention of the telescope.

Then on 23 February 1987 came another, an explosion 160,000 light-years away in a satellite galaxy of our own, known as the 'Large Magellanic Cloud'.

 A giant supernova, one of the heaven's most spectacular and rarest astronomical events, formed by the collapse and explosion of a massive star.

EDGE OF SPACE

It is almost impossible to state precisely where the Earth's atmosphere ends and space begins. It could be anywhere in a region between 1,000 km (621 miles) and 3,200 km (1,988 miles) above Earth.

In terms of the history of space flight, the frontier could be considered to be at 160 km (99 miles), where the atmosphere becomes tenuous and the laws of aerodynamics give way to those of astrodynamics.

SHUTTLE GLOW

The space shuttle and many satellites orbit at altitudes of 250-300 km (155-186 miles) – about twenty-five times as high as commercial jet aircraft fly. The shuttle speeds through the thin gases, composed of atomic oxygen and molecular nitrogen, at a speed of eight kilometres per second (5 miles/sec) which causes the air to rush past the spacecraft, like wind around a speeding car. The impact of this wind on the surface of the shuttle causes some parts of the spacecraft to glow and others to be eroded away.

ASTRONAUTS & COSMONAUTS

The first woman in space was Valentina Tereshkova who flew in *Vostok 6* in June 1983, completing forty-eight revolutions of the Earth and spending seventy hours and fifty minutes in space.

After her mission she married Cosmonaut Nikolayev. They had two children who had the distinction of being the first children both of whose parents had been into space.

The next time a woman went into space was 1983.

It would have been the first manned Apollo mission. Instead, Virgil 'Gus' Grissom, Edward H. White and Roger B. Chaffee became the first astronauts to die in a spacecraft, on 27 January 1967. A fire broke out while they were sitting in the *Apollo* capsule, atop the Saturn launch vehicle at the Kennedy Space Centre. Within fifteen seconds the three were dead and the fire was out.

No definitive cause was found for the fire but an electrical short-circuit was the most likely. The fierceness of the blaze was put down to the fact that *Apollo* spacecraft had a one hundred per cent oxygen atmosphere.

The first European to fly in space was Czechoslovak cosmonaut, Vladimir Remek in March 1978 on the *Soyuz 27* mission.

The first Belgian in space was Dirk Fremont, an electronics scientist, who was one of a seven-man crew for Mission STS45 on the space shuttle *Atlantis* in March 1992.

MEN ON THE MOON

For the record, the first words of Neil Armstrong when he opened the hatch door to step down onto the moon were: 'I'm gonna step off the LEM now...(Pause)...That's one small step for man, one giant leap for mankind...(Longer pause)...The surface is fine and powdery. I can pick it up loosely with my toe...'

Pierre Cardin, the famous French fashion designer, claimed that his greatest achievement 'was probably walking in the same space suit Armstrong used on the moon. No other human has done that. NASA at Houston said, "It's forbidden" at first. Then they let me. The suit has six thicknesses, it's most bizarre, like wearing another body.' He said it felt 'light, very light indeed.'

ASTRONAUT'S TOOL KIT

The astronaut's tool kit, designed for the first lunar landing, incorporated new devices for making repairs in the zero gravity of space. These included a

Spammer (space hammer), a *Plench* (pliers and wrench), a *Zert* (zero-reaction tool), and the *Nab* (not and blot), a special wrench permitting the astronaut to apply twisting-force to a bolt without moving his body.

PIONEER PLAQUE

Two engraved plaques were placed aboard the spacecraft *Pioneer 10* and *Pioneer 11*, the first of mankind's artefacts that will escape the solar system and travel forever through the galaxies at a speed of around sixteen kilometres per second (10 miles/sec.)

Each plaque is made of gold-anodized aluminium and measures 15 x 23 cm (6 x 9 in). They show a chart of the nine planets of our solar system, the location of earth, the time the spacecraft was launched and its track through space, the figures of a man and a woman and other essential data. They will survive for hundreds of millions of years in space, a 'cosmic greeting card' designed to communicate with other life forms – if they exist out there.

THE VOYAGER RECORD

A special record was placed on board the two *Voyager* spacecraft before their launch to the outer reaches of the solar system and beyond.

Each twelve-inch copper disc contain greetings from Earth people in sixty languages and samples of music from different cultures and eras, including *Johnny B. Goode* by Chuck Berry, a Pygmy girl's initiation song and the *Brandenburg Concerto*.

This is followed by '*A Sound Essay on the Evolution of Planet Earth*' which includes natural sounds of surf, wind and thunder, birds, whales and other animals, laughter, morse code, a train whistle, a kiss, the lift-off of a *Saturn* rocket and the sounds of a baby.

There are 115 pictures on the disc including views of the Taj Mahal, a supermarket, the Great Wall of China, human sex organs, a tree toad and a group of sprinters.

It also contains electronic information that an advanced technological civilisation could convert into diagrams, pictures and printed words, including a message from the then President, Jimmy Carter.

Both records are housed in protective aluminium jackets which means they are likely to survive for more than a billion years. Thus it represents not only a message in space but also a message in time.

The *Voyager* missions, which have contributed more to our understanding of the planets than 3,000 years of earthbound observations, cost each US citizen just $2.40.

SATURN V

The *Saturn V* was the most powerful rocket booster ever flown, weighing 2.8 million kg (6.2 million lb) and standing 110 m (363 ft) tall. The building in which it was assembled – The Vehicle Assembly Building – is 160 m (526 ft) high, so high in fact that it had to be fully air-conditioned to prevent clouds forming in the ceiling and rusting the Moon rockets.

When the *Saturn V* was launched 'all up' for the first time, the sound volume was compared to the eruption of the volcano Krakatoa in 1883. The pressure wave generated by the first-stage engines was detected 1,770 km (1,100 miles) away.

SOLAR SAILING

Spacecraft of the future may be powered by sunlight. Since the mid-1960s space scientists have been exploring the possibilities of the solar sail – an extremely thin sheet of reflective material as large as a football field, held in tension by wires and struts.

The 'wind' in the rigging of a solar sail is light emanating from the Sun. As it is reflected off the sail, it transfers some of its momentum to it. This momentum can either slow the craft down or speed it up, depending on the sail's orientation to the Sun. It becomes possible to steer the craft by changing the angle of the sail.

A solar sail could carry a payload as heavy as a truck or transport supplies to manned colonies on other planets. In the future, it may also be possible to stage solar sail races between the planets.

MURDER IN SPACE

There will be money to be made from lawsuits in space, according to a 1986 report from a US law school. The most comprehensive existing law is the 1967 Outer Space Treaty but this would not cover, for instance, the death of an astronaut in orbit. Professor Ralph Steinhardt of the George Washington University Law School predicts: 'In thirty or forty years we're going to have our first murder in outer space.'

ASTRONOMY

In 1987, a dead fly put one of the telescopes at the Royal Greenwich Observatory out of action.

The fly got inside the telescope and, before expiring, broke the cross-wires that enable astronomers to align the telescope and locate stars accurately in the centre of its field of view.

The irony about it is that the cross-wires are made of thin strands from a spider's web, a practice first started in the nineteenth century.

The problem was that there was no-one at the observatory who was skilled enough to select the right spider's web and make replacement cross-wires from it.

Astronomers at Jodrell Bank admitted in January 1992 that the planet they 'discovered' the year before – the first ever found outside our solar system – was an illusion, caused by a tiny error in their calculations.

The scientists had hypothesised the existence of a planet ten times the mass of Earth to explain a cyclical variation in the signals coming from a pulsar. They had failed to take into account the slight variation in the orbit of the Earth and had located the pulsar one-tenth of a degree off its true position.

One of the scientists commented: 'At least we hadn't got around to giving it a name.'

Subsequently, two American astronomers have discovered what they believe to be two planets outside our solar system, in orbit around a collapsed star. Their calculations have been verified. If correct, this means planet-making is an even more common activity than previously thought.

IS ANYBODY OUT THERE ?

The Milky Way contains 400 billion stars. Ten billion of these might be expected to have potentially habitable planets. If life evolved on only one in a thousand of them, there would be ten million civilisations within 130,000 light years. The odds appear to be in favour of extraterrestrial intelligence.

Steven Spielberg, the director of *E.T.*, donated $100,000 to the costs of a search by scientists at Harvard University for intelligent life in the universe.

A ten-year, $100 million NASA programme – the Search for Extraterrestrial Intelligence (SETI) was launched on 12 October 1992, the 500th anniversary of Columbus's discovery of the New World.

There are two aspects to SETI; one radio telescope at Arecibo in Puerto Rico will target 1,000 nearby stars; other telescopes will conduct a continuous skysweep of the rest.

The clever part is the analysis of the data. Special computer chips have been designed that can analyze millions of frequencies simultaneously.

The SETI Continuous Wave Signal Computer can make one billion tests per second for intelligent signals; the equivalent of scanning the *Encyclopaedia Britannica* in one second, and picking out a specific three-word phrase.

VERNE'S VISIONS

Extraordinary parallels exist between the journey in Jules Verne's *From The Earth to the Moon*, written in 1865, and the *Apollo 11* moon-landing flight in 1969.

Verne's spacecraft was launched from Cape Town, Florida, a site near the present launch facility at Cape Canaveral.

There were three men in his ship, which was called the *Columbiad*; there were three men in the Apollo command module, named *Columbia*.

Verne's craft travelled at about 40,000 km per hour (25,000 mph) and reached the moon in four days and one hour; Apollo travelled at 38,600 km per hour (24,000 mph) and made the trip in four days and six hours.

Verne foresaw the possibility of his fictional voyage becoming reality. He wrote: 'What one man can imagine, another can do.'

FAST FOOD

The McDonald's empire was founded by Ray Kroc who, by the time he died on 14 January 1984, at the age of eighty-one, had made the company into the world's leading fast-food chain with more than 7,500 outlets in the US and thirty-one other countries.

The company is constantly searching for new locations. Its strategy is based on 'The Monotony Index' which states that, the higher the level of monotony in a town, the better McDonald's chance of doing business there.

According to Ray Kroc's autobiography called, appropriately enough, *Grinding It Out*, he had a job selling milk-shake machines and was intrigued to hear that one restaurant in San Bernadino, California, was using eight of these machines simultaneously. When he drove out there one fateful day in 1954, he discovered the McDonald brothers running a drive-in restaurant selling hamburgers and other fast food. He came away clutching a contract to franchise McDonald's across America and subsequently bought the brothers out for $2.7 million.

The McDonald's Big Mac hamburger is the perfect universal currency because exactly the same product is served up world-wide.

Colonel Harland Sanders worked as a locomotive fireman, steamboat ferry operator, lawyer, tyre salesman, petrol station operator, farm-hand, insurance salesman, street car conductor and served as a soldier in Cuba before opening first a snack bar and then a roadside restaurant. His title was an honorary one, very common in Kentucky.

When he was sixty-five, Colonel Sanders invented the fast-frying process for cooking chicken and the coating, containing eighteen herbs and spices, that led to his world-wide fame. He franchised the idea and his name to 400 outlets before selling out his interests in 1964 for one million pounds.

On his eighty-eighth birthday in 1978, the Kentucky Fried Chicken Corporation celebrated by inviting 800 guests to a roast beef dinner, followed by the opening of a chicken museum at the company's corporate headquarters.

It is believed that the Colonel died, aged ninety of leukaemia.

COLA

Coca-Cola was originally a medicine, invented in May 1886, by John Styth Pemberton, a former Confederate officer-turned patent medicine supplier.

When prohibition was declared in the Southern States, he removed the wine from his French Wine Coca – 'Ideal Brain Tonic' and added extracts of kola nut (a stimulant brought over by the slaves) and coca, plus assorted oils and flavourings to make a new drink. It was originally called 'Intellectual Beverage and Temperance Drink'.

The Coca-Cola name and logo came from his business partner Frank M. Robinson. Pemberton subsequently sold out his interests to one, Willis Venable, credited with inventing the idea of adding soda water to the drink.

The secret formula of Coca-Cola is known as 'Merchandise 7X' and is one of the best-kept secrets in American industry, known only to a handful of trusted employees. It is preserved in written form in a security vault in Georgia.

When the Coca Cola company introduced a new logo in 1969, it launched 'Project Arden', named after the cosmetics company. This involved replacing the logo on every delivery vehicle in the world's second largest truck fleet (after the US postal service) and replacing an estimated eighteen million Coke signs around the world.

Pepsi-Cola was invented by Caleb B. Babraham, a pharmacist who constructed a beverage known originally as 'Brad's Drink', a name he changed to Pepsi-Cola in 1893.

During the war in Cambodia, the government commandeered Pepsi's 110 trucks and they became popular targets for Viet Cong rockets. The word 'Pepsi' became associated with the explosion that resulted when a rocket hit a truck loaded with hand grenades or with cases of warm soda.

BIG FOOD

When a 400 kg (900 lb) pancake was prepared for a hungry crowd at a fair in Highgate, Vermont, USA, the ingredients were churned in a cement mixer and the pancake was flipped by helicopter.

Periodically, the villagers of Denby Dale in West Yorkshire bake a giant pie to mark some celebration or other.

The custom began in 1788 to celebrate King George III's reported recovery from insanity; two weeks later, he was certified insane again. The second pie was baked to mark the Duke of Wellington's victory at Waterloo.

In 1846 the third pie, baked to celebrate the repeal of the Corn Laws,

 Six-year-old Billy Sicklemore prepares to sink his teeth into a giant sandwich at an event in 1992 to celebrate the invention of the snack.

required thirteen horses to pull it through the town. It contained five sheep, one calf, a hundred pounds of beef, fourteen rabbits, seven hares, two brace each of pheasant and partridge, two guinea fowl, two ducks, two turkeys, two geese, six pigeons, four hens and sixty-three small birds.

As a recent mayor of the village commented, they appeared to have shot everything that passed through the village except horses and people.

In 1887, the Great Jubilee Pie, when opened, 'emitted such an intolerable stench that a number of persons were injured in the stampede to escape.' As soon as the smell had died down, the odious concoction was buried in quick lime and a successful 'Resurrection Pie' was baked in its place.

The 1964 pie was baked to commemorate four royal births in one year. That contained three tons of beef, one and a half tons of potatoes and over half a ton of gravy and seasoning. It fed 30,000 people and the proceeds raised were used to build a Pie Hall community centre, outside which stands the steel dish – 5.5 m long x 1.8 m wide x 0.5 m deep (18 ft long x 6 ft wide x 18 in) deep – in which it was baked.

The ninth pie, the last one baked in the village to date – was another monster meat and potato pie – made to celebrate the bicentenary of the first pie. Some villagers felt the event should have been postponed until the time came to celebrate the coronation of King Charles III.

DIGESTIVES

McVitie's Digestives were first sold in 1892 and to mark its centenary, the company published a commemorative newspaper, the *Daily Digestive*.

The Company was founded by William McVitie, a failed writer who was a friend of both Rabbie Burns and Sir Walter Scott, who named a character in *Ivanhoe* after him.

His grandson, Robert was running the business in 1887 when a baker called Alexander Grant joined the firm; five years later, Grant came up with the Digestive that made the company's fortune.

It got its name because the baking soda in it was thought to be good for indigestion. The word biscuit, incidentally, comes from the Medieval French *bis cuit*, meaning twice cooked; bread was first baked, then sliced, then baked again so that it would keep on a long voyage).

In 1902 the company began building a factory in Harlesden, London which is still producing biscuits. They were originally mixed by hand, by hundreds of women using huge mixing bowls. Once a week, Alexander Grant travelled third class overnight on the train from Glasgow with only a set of biscuit-cutters in his suitcase.

The Harlesden plant is now the second-biggest biscuit factory in the world (after Nabisco's plant in Chicago), the largest in Europe and the most automated anywhere.

McVities has a turnover of more than two million pounds, owns a string of other companies, and is now called, United Biscuits.

Britons eat five million digestive biscuits every day.

ONE MAN'S MEAT

Americans eat 110% more beef today per person that they did in 1925. Beefsteaks and prime ribs are seldom eaten by people outside the US and a few other affluent countries.

India has about one-fifth of all the world's cattle but Hindus don't eat beef as they are too highly-valued as sources of power, producers of milk and as religious symbols.

Horsemeat is the preferred meat in Mongolia and many parts of Central Asia. It's popular in China and Japan and out-sells mutton and lamb, combined in Sweden.

For centuries the Chinese have reared special breeds of dog, such as the black-tongued Chow, for eating. The Mexican Hairless dog was the principal food of the Aztecs. Dog-eating was widespread among the American Indian tribes of the Central Plains and California. Dog-meat is also eaten in parts of the Pacific islands of Hawaii and Central Samoa.

When British and American explorers first reached Hawaii, the islanders were baffled by the fact that the white men thought it wrong to eat dog but not pig, as they kept both as household pets. Captain Cook ate and enjoyed dogmeat.

In Hong Kong and Taiwan, dog is sold under the name, 'fragrant meat'.

Guinea pigs provide perhaps fifty per cent of all the protein eaten in Peru.

In West Africa, the cane rat, the giant rat and the common house mouse provide much-needed protein.

Animal milk is not used as food throughout large areas of Laos, Vietnam, Cambodia, Thailand, and China, nor among some of the peoples of India. The Malays and Burmese drink little milk. In Africa, many tribes restrict milk-drinking to certain classes of people.

INSECT-EATING

According to *African Insect Recipes*, by Martha Wapensky, the correct way to cook the African Fried Flying Ant is as follows: 'Fry the ants in a dray pan. Remove the pan, dry the ants in the sun and winnow out wings and any stones. Fry the ants again, with or without a little oil, add bit of salt and cook until done. Serve with rice.'

In Mexico there are 2,346 potentially nutritious types of insect. The termite apparently has four-times the calorific value of beef. Caterpillars, cactus worms and grasshoppers taste of nuts fried in butter, pork and shrimp respectively.

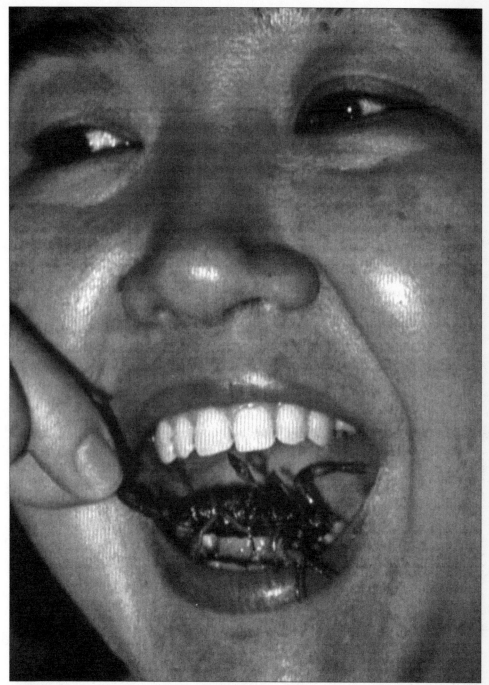

 Deep—fried scorpions are best eaten with the poison intact. The Chinese believe it's a cure for spasms, boils and nervous convulsions.

The French astronomer, Josephe-Jerome de Lalande used to enjoy spreading spiders on bread and butter

A sample menu in the classic work, *Why Not Eat Insects?* by Vincent M. Holt, originally published in 1885, consists of the following: for starters, either slug soup or boiled cod with snail sauce; main courses provide a choice of four dishes – wasp grubs fried in the comb, moths sautéed in butter, braised beef with caterpillars or new carrots with wire worm sauce; for dessert, either gooseberry cream with sawflies, devilled chafer grubs, or stag beetle larvae on toast.

In 1986 in eastern Thailand, two students won first prize in a contest designed to promote pest control and protect crops, by eating more than 900 gm (2 lb) of fried locusts in five minutes.

The previous year in Bangkok, a Thai building worker who ate four bags of locusts as a snack, died of insecticide poisoning.

In 1992, the New York Entomological Society celebrated its centennial with a banquet which included on the menu, chocolate cricket torte, mealworm ganoush, wax worm fritters with plum sauce and other such delights. Honeypot ants, their abdomens distended with peach nectar, were generally considered a hit, although most guest passed on the three-inch sautéed Thai water bugs which looked too similar to giant cockroaches.

The after-dinner talk was given by Gene DeFoliart, editor of the *Food Insects Newsletter*, on the virtues of 'entomophagy', as its more poshly called.

He told the assembled guests that people throughout the world eat at least some insects. At cinemas in Colombia, for example, roasted ants are eaten like popcorn. In some parts of Africa, more than sixty per cent of villagers' protein comes from insects.

GEOPHAGY

Strange cravings for unusual foods, a condition that most commonly occurs among pregnant women, is called *pica*, from the Latin word for magpie. But the most extraordinary and widespread form of pica is 'geophagy', the habit of eating earth.

Geophagy is practised by millions, most commonly in West Africa and the southern states of the US. In just one village north of Accra, the capital of Ghana, some five thousand tons of rock are mined each year and turned into food. The clay is crushed, sieved and mixed with water into a dough, which is then rolled into a distinctive shape which becomes a trademark for the village.

In Mississippi, people cheerfully admit to being 'earth eaters' and consider it a tasty snack. The fine, brown earth has a texture a bit like sherbet and ranges in taste, from sweet and chalky to sour and metallic.

In Africa, it is believed the habit survives due to its original purpose – to provide a valuable mineral supplement. In America it has a more malignant origin. Slaves ate earth in response to fear, panic and starvation and often became fatally addicted; they would eat so much earth that their gut and bowels would get blocked.

TRUFFLES

Truffles are the underground, fruiting bodies of fungi. They form irregular spheres and take about seven years to reach their mature size of around ten centimetres (4 in). The largest recorded to date was a two kilogram (4 lb) white truffle found in Italy in the early 1950s, which was given to the then US President, Harry S. Truman.

There are about 200 varieties found on virtually all continents, even in the sands of the Arabian peninsula. Not all of them are edible, many taste hideous and a few are mildly poisonous. The only species of interest to gourmets are found in small areas of Italy, France and Spain.

 A fine example of the truffle, one of the world's most expensive foods. Few are found and most are eaten in their country of origin, so the small number that reach the gourmet restaurants fetch high prices.

The black, Perigord truffle costs more than $880 per kg ($400 per lb); the rarer white truffle up to $2,330 per kg ($1,060 per lb). They remain in peak edible condition for only a week.

People used to think that truffles were either caused by insects stinging the roots of trees or as a result of thunderbolts. We now know that truffles grow only in symbiosis with the roots of particular trees, an arrangement that benefits both organisms. Hornbeam and poplar, hazel and oak are favoured hosts for the gourmet varieties.

Truffles are rare and therefore very costly. Few are found, most are eaten in their country of origin and a small proportion find their way to restaurants in the rest of the world.

The reason so few are found is that you never know where they will grow from year to year. They must be hunted down with dogs or pigs, who can smell a ripe truffle under forty-five centimetres (18 in) of earth. Bears were even used for this purpose in the last century. The reason that these animals are attracted to them is that truffles contain a steroid that is also produced by boars before mating; the steroid acts as a *pheromone* – a hormone produced by one animal which serves as a chemical message to communicate with another. This also attracts the small animals like squirrels that eat the truffles and disperse their spores.

Truffles are rare and getting rarer, mainly due to the loss of their host trees. In 1925 the annual truffle harvest was about 450 tons; in 1986 it was just twenty tons.

A French company has analyzed the unique aroma of truffles, a blend of at least fourteen compounds, and produced an artificial truffle oil. They have also developed an electronic truffle-sniffer. Many others are working on ways of cultivating truffles artificially, with only modest success so far.

FANTASTIC BODIES!

INGREDIENTS

There are about 100 trillion cells in the human body. Each minute, 300 million of them die. If they were not constantly renewed, all your body-cells would be dead in about 230 days.

Water constitutes sixty-one per cent of the body – about 47 litres (50 quarts) in an average man. About 2.4 litres (2½ quarts) are lost each day through exhalation, perspiration and excretion. Water makes up between twenty and eighty per cent of most bodily tissues, and as much as eighty-five per cent of brain tissue. If all the water were drained from a man weighing 73 kg (160 lb), his dehydrated remains would weigh only 29 kg (64 lb).

Besides water, the body contains an assortment of other substances. On average, it has: enough lime to whitewash a small shed; enough fat to make seven large bars of soap; enough sugar to fill a jam jar; enough salt to fill six salt cellars; enough carbon 13 kg (28.7 lb) to make 9,000 pencil leads; enough phosphorous to make 2,200 match-heads; enough iron to make a twenty-five millimetre (1 inch) nail; a spoonful of sulphur and 30 gm (1 oz) of other metals.

BLOOD

It has been calculated that the blood cells in a human body, if arranged in single file, would measure a staggering 96,500 km (59,000 miles) – enough to stretch comfortably twice around the world.

Fifty per cent of a single pinprick of blood contains five million red corpuscles (or cells), 10,000 white corpuscles and 250,000 platelets. The other half consists of a watery substance called, plasma.

One red cell takes about ten seconds to travel from your heart to your head and back again, and about one minute to travel to your big toe and back. In one day it travels round the body more than a thousand times. Each red cell lives for about 120 days.

Human red blood corpuscles are created by bone marrow at the rate of about 1.2 million corpuscles per second. In a lifetime, the bone marrow creates about half a tonne of corpuscles.

'Bleeding' used to be considered a cure for all manner of ailments. Frederick The Great demanded that his veins be opened during battles, to soothe his nerves. Louis XIII of France underwent forty-seven bleedings in six months.

HEART

Our hearts beat from sixty to seventy times every minute of our lives. This works out at between 2-3,000 million beats in an average life span. The heart forces blood around 96,560 km (60,000 miles) of internal pipes – a plumbing system that is longer than the road networks of Wales and Scotland put together. The smallest pipes – of which there are billions – have a combined surface area of 8,000 sq m (2 acres).

Even during sleep, the fist-sized heart of an adult pumps about 340 litres (75 gals) an hour – enough to fill an average car's petrol tank every seven minutes. It generates enough muscle-power every day to lift an average-sized car about 15 m (50 ft).

Blood takes fifty to sixty seconds to travel on its circular journey through the heart. The heart beat is not the noise of the muscles contracting. In fact, what we hear is the noise of the heart's valves being forced to slam shut.

The bigger the animal, the slower its heart beat. A human baby's heart beats about 130 times a minute. At three years old, it beats about 100 times a minute, at twelve, about 90 times. An adult's heart beats around seventy times a minute. During an average life, the heart beats at least 2,500 million times. In that time, it will pump around 500 million litres (110 million gallons) of blood.

LUNGS

There are said to be 300,000 million capillary vessels in the lungs. They would stretch 2,400 km (1,500 miles) if laid end to end.

A human can live without food for five weeks, without water for five days, but for only five minutes without air.

Our lungs can contain around nine milk bottles-worth of air – a massive five litres (1.3 gals) – although we only breathe a fraction of that under normal circumstances.

In twenty-four hours at rest, you take in enough air to fill around three telephone boxes and, on a normal day, you breathe in enough to fill six.

STOMACH

The first direct look that anyone had at the workings of the stomach was in 1822. A man called, Alexius St Martin was shot in the left side. The hole only partially healed and a certain Dr William Beaumont used this to his advantage.

He dangled various foods on silk threads into the man's stomach to see what happened. The patient got tired of this and ran away. He married, had children and lived to be 82.

INTESTINE

Coiled up like a hose-pipe inside our bodies, the small intestine is six to seven metres (20-23 ft) long. This is equivalent to the height of the tallest giraffe, or four times the length of the nose of the Statue of Liberty.

It is lined with finger-like projections called *villi* from a Latin word meaning, 'shaggy hair'. If all five million of these, each the size of a comma, were laid out flat they would cover an area of nine square metres (100 sq ft). This is approximately five times the area of the skin – around the size of two table-tennis tables.

KIDNEYS

Our two kidneys, which weigh around 142 gm (5 oz) each, contain 1,250,000 'nephrons' (filter units) in each one. An average of about 1.3 litres (2.2 pints) of blood are pumped through the kidneys every minute of our lives – a total of 180 litres (48 gals) during a normal day. The kidneys make 1.4 litres (2.5 pints) of urine out of it, which we pass in the average day. If you lived to be seventy, that's a total of 38,325 litres (10,000 gallons).

BONES

Bone is a mixture of organic and mineral matter; a fibrous protein called *collagen* and tiny crystals of calcium phosphate, which form a mineral known as *apatite*.

If you remove the apatite by dipping a bone in acid, it becomes so rubbery, you can tie it in a knot. On the other hand, if the collagen is destroyed, the bone becomes extremely brittle. The minerals give bone its hardness but the collagen gives it strength.

The word, skeleton is derived from the Greek word for 'dried-up'.

Before we are born and during childhood, our bones are much softer than they are in adulthood. This is because they consist of cartilage, which is tough and rubbery but not solid like bone, which it gradually changes into. Your bones are not fully hard until you are about twenty-five years old. This process is called 'ossification'.

After ossification, bone is made up of seventy per cent hard, non-living matter and thirty per cent living matter. Some cartilage never turns into bone: examples are the rings in your neck which hold the breathing tube open, your nose and your ears.

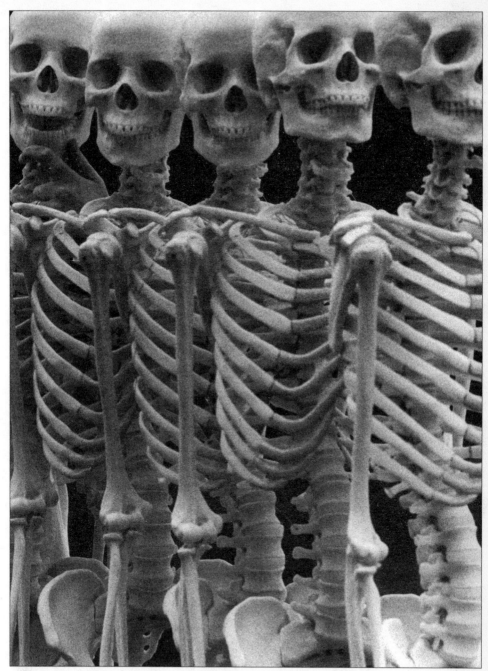

 FACT For many years, the world's largest exporter of human bones was the Reknas Company in Calcutta, India, which pioneered bulk sales of skeletons.

Most people have twelve pairs of ribs. One in twenty people have thirteen pairs. A few people have only eleven pairs.

We have about 206 strong, hollow bones in our bodies and yet a typical adult skeleton of a 73 kg (160 lb)-body weighs less than 4 kg (9 lb). The same framework in steel would be four or five times as heavy. Human bone is as strong as granite in supporting weight. A block the size of a matchbox can support nine tonnes – four times as much as concrete.

At birth, human babies have some 350 bones, more than one-and a half times the number they will have as adults. Many of the small bones in the infant skeleton eventually fuse to form larger ones.

A giraffe has the same number of vertebrae in its neck as we have, although its neck is much longer.

GROWING PAINS

The body grows about a third of an inch every night, but shrinks to its original size the next day. This is because, when the body is prone, the cartilage disks of the spine are relieved of gravity's downward pull and expand, adding to body length.

Recent findings suggest that new-born babies can go for up to sixty-three days without growing and will then suddenly grow in spurts, putting on half an inch in up to twenty-four hours. This process requires furious cell production – just before this happens, babies become very cranky, fussy and extremely hungry. Parents be warned.

MUSCLES

Picking up a pencil uses at least twelve pairs of muscles. Taking a step uses more than 200 pairs. You use forty-three muscles to frown but only seventeen to smile.

About forty per cent of the weight of a man and thirty-five per cent of the weight of a woman is muscle. There are well over 600 muscles in the body.

The biggest muscle in the human body is the 'gluteus maximus' (the bottom); the smallest – 0.12 cm (½ in) long – is attached to the smallest bone of the body, inside the ear.

SKIN

The thickness of the skin varies. On the eyelids it's only half a millimetre (¹⁄₅₀ inch). On the soles of the feet, it's half a centimetre (even thicker if you usually walk barefoot). Average skin-thickness is one to two millimetres.

Each square inch of human skin consists of nineteen million cells, sixty hairs, ninety oil glands, nineteen feet of blood vessels, 625 sweat glands and 19,000 sensory cells.

The skin is the body's largest organ. In an adult man, it covers about 1.9 sq m (20 sq ft); a woman has about 1.6 sq m (17 sq ft). The skin of the human adult weighs 2.7 kg (6 lb).

On average, each person sheds about 18 kg (40 lb) of skin during his or her lifetime.

Eighty per cent of household dust is actually dead skin.

BRAIN

The brain has some 12,000 million nerve cells. Scientist Colin Blakemore has calculated that, if the nerve cells and fibres in one human brain were stretched end to end they would reach the moon and back, as each cubic inch of the cerebral cortex (the grey matter that makes up the main part of the two hemispheres of the brain) contains 16,000 km (10,000 miles) of nerve fibres, connecting the cells together.

The brain is a soft, greyish lump that looks like a large, wrinkled walnut. It weighs about one and a half kilograms (3.3 lb).

The brain accounts for about three per cent of body weight. But it uses twenty per cent of all the oxygen we breathe, twenty per cent of the calories in the food we eat and about fifteen per cent of the body's total blood supply.

Brain injuries often provide powerful insights into the mysteries of human thought and memory.

One such recent case, reported in the scientific literature of 1992, concerns a seventy year-old retired librarian who, as the result of a brain injury, lost the ability to name animals, although she could still name other living things, such as plants or inanimate objects. She couldn't describe the physical attributes of animals either, (when asked, for example, 'what colour is a whale'?) But she could remember whether a particular animal lived on land or sea, or was wild or domesticated.

This shows that the brain has different ways of classifying different kinds of information. One is language-based, and one, sight-based; one can be destroyed while the other stays intact.

Louis Pasteur, who suffered a haemorrhage on the left side of his brain, was able to function for the rest of his life with no great discomfort or loss of mental power.

In 1848, engineer, Phineas Gage was attempting to blast a rock while working on the railroad. He was using an iron rod, one metre (3 1/2 ft) long and 5.8 kg (13 lb) in weight, to tamp-down explosives. The rod blew back at him with terrific force and went straight through his skull, below the left eye, and emerged from the back of his head.

Astonishingly, he recovered quickly with his eyesight, speech and senses intact. But a small portion of his brain had been damaged by the accident – resulting in a change of character. Before the accident he had been well-known as a pleasant individual. Afterwards, he became ill-tempered and violent and unable to hold on to his job. He was reduced to exhibiting himself as a fairground attraction. His skull and the iron bar that injured him are now on display at Harvard Medical School in the USA.

A retired English film-studio manager, John Clogg, is a man in a thousand million with a very rare brain condition known as 'double hemisphere action'. As a result he can simultaneously write different sentences with his right and left hands and carry on a quite unconnected conversation. Leonardo da Vinci is believed to have had the same ability, but Clogg says his talent has never been a bit of use to him.

The term 'brainwashing' was first used by American journalist, Edward Hunter during the Korean war.

The first electrical experiments on the brain were carried out by two medical officers of the Prussian army after the Battle of Sedan in 1870. Officers Fritsch and Hitzig went over the battlefield, testing their 'galvanic current' on exposed brains. They found that, when stimulated by the current, certain areas at the side of the brain produced movements in the opposite side of the body.

EYES

As much as a third of our cerebral cortex, the 'highest' level in our brains, is devoted to visual processing. Our eyes are connected to the optic nerves by two million fibres; by comparison, our auditory nerves only contain 30,000 fibres.

The retina of the eye consists of millions of nerve-endings that are sensitive to light. These light receptors are of two types: rods and cones. Rods are concerned with black and white vision; cones with colour vision.

The retina contains about 130 million rods and seven million cones, which pass 'information' to the brain through the optic nerve – a stalk consisting of some 800,000 nerve fibres.

At least a quarter of the human race is short-sighted. One hundred million Americans wear glasses or contact lenses. Every year, some 100,000 Americans go blind.

Colour blindness is probably caused by faulty cones. About eight per cent of males are affected, but few females are because it is a condition determined by the genes in the 'X' chromosome.

The eye of a male is slightly bigger than that of a female; a woman's eye shows a higher proportion of white than a man's.

TEARS

Tears contain an enzyme called 'lysozyme', which kills bacteria and protects the eye from infection.

Sufferers from a rare illness known as, Sjogren's Syndrome (which attacks the tear glands), cannot cry.

The First World Congress on Tears was held in Dallas, Texas in 1986. Scientists reported on the fact that there is a marked chemical difference between tears caused by unhappiness and those caused by onions.

HAIR

Oriental people have more head-hairs than any other race – about 120,000. Afro-Caribbeans have an average of 110,000. A Caucasian blonde has 140,000, a brown-haired person has 108,000 and the average redhead, a mere 90,000.

Each individual hair has an independent life cycle. At any one time, ninety per cent of the hairs in our scalp are growing at the rate of about twelve millimetres (½ inch) each month and ten per cent are dormant. These remain inactive for three months before dropping out. We lose 50-100 head-hairs every day.

Eyelashes do not become white with age like other head and body hairs. Each eye has around 200 lashes. There are more on the upper lid than the lower. Each lasts between three to five months before falling out and being replaced – the same life span as the hair of the eyebrows.

SHAVING

If a man starts shaving at the age of eighteen and spends ten minutes a day removing his stubble – he will have dedicated 2,555 hours, or 106 days to his chin by the time he's sixty years old.

FACT Lots of people have pony tails but this fantasy hairstyle is definitely taking things one jump too far.

MOUTH

A healthy person's mouth may harbour more than forty species of bacteria, as well as a number of viruses, fungi and protozoans.

Saliva can contain as many as a billion streptococci per millilitre and there are around one hundred bacteria on every cell in the tongue.

There are about 9000 taste buds on the tongue, with some additional ones on the linings of the cheek and the pharynx. They can detect four main tastes – sweet, bitter, sour and salt. All other tastes are mixtures of these four.

Not all tasting takes place here. There are sweet and salt taste buds in other parts of the mouth and upper throat, and sour and bitter tastes are detected on the roof of the mouth where the hard and the soft palate meet.

Dentists still fill 25 million teeth every year in Britain alone.

According to a Chinese newspaper article, published in Beijing in 1992, a kiss takes three minutes off your life because it speeds up and increases the pressure on your heart. Just 175,200 kisses and you've lost a year. Another paper responded, stating that kissing could prolong your life, was beneficial to your teeth and excellent for slimmers, burning off three calories per smooch.

ARTIFICIAL MOUTH

Scientists at New Zealand's Dental Research Unit have constructed a fifty cm (20 in)-long glass mouth. Inside, instead of teeth, are 'plaque growth stations' on which bacteria are fed a diet of false saliva. The artificial mouth sits inside an incubator to keep warm. After a few weeks, it develops bad breath – a stench like rancid butter – which the scientists combat with deodorisers. The mouth is designed to help researchers study the growth of plaque and try treatments for tooth decay.

 This 1978 portrait of the diminutive strongman Ivan Karl from Northampton, shows him checking his 'tooth grip' before he has to lift two showgirls with his teeth as part of his circus act.

SNORING

There is now an operation available to cure heavy snoring. Snoring is caused by vibrations of the mouth's palate. Surgeons use a laser to slightly burn the palate – as the burn heals, it forms scar tissue which stiffens the palate. The operation takes five minutes, patients are discharged within twenty-four hours and, apart from sore throats, suffer no serious side-effects.

NOSE

The nose supplies the lungs with over fourteen cubic metres (500 cu ft) of conditioned air, every twenty-four hours. The lungs need dust-free air at a temperature of 35 °C (95 °F) and ninety-five per cent humidity .

Inside the nose are 'mucous membranes' which secrete two pints of water a day and in which are embedded millions of tiny hairs called, 'cilia', which beat at a rate of 250 times a minute. The mucous is gradually moved by them and the forces of gravity to the back of the throat where it is swallowed.

Smelling is carried out by two patches about the size of a small coin, containing five million yellowish cells, situated high up the nasal passages. A dog, by contrast, has 220 million of these cells.

One sneeze can shoot 20,000 droplets of moisture four metres away.

The world's most powerful sneezers have been timed to discover the fastest sneeze on earth. The world record for a sneeze is 166 km per hour (103 mph).

SMELL TESTERS

To test the effectiveness of deodorants, many companies employ 'assessors' whose job it is to spend their working days sniffing other people's armpits.

In a typical test, a team of volunteers, male and female, have their armpits sprayed or rolled with the test product. A number of hours later, they return to be sniffed by the assessors.

The assessors' sense of smell is so acute, they claim to be able to detect, by the smell of sweat what a person had for dinner the night before. The pong-level (known as 'malodour' in the trade) is assessed on a scale of one to five.

Sweat itself does not smell, it is the bacteria breakdown that produces body odour.

Each armpit sweats a different amount.

ELBOW

The word, elbow comes from the combination of two other words – 'ell' and 'bend'. An ell was an old form of measurement which equalled two cubits (a cubit was the length of the forearm).

The phrase, ' hitting one's funny bone' is a pun on the technical term for the humerus, the bone of the upper arm.

FINGERS & HANDS

The fingers bend and stretch at least 25 million times during the course of an average lifetime.

 Two smell testers get a tough assignment. There must be some worse jobs, but not many.

Ten per cent of the population is left-handed. On average, left-handers die younger than right-handed people.

Leonardo da Vinci, Michelangelo, Pablo Picasso, Benjamin Franklin and Charlie Chaplin were all left-handed.

A staggering fifty-four per cent of all premature babies are left handed.

FEET

Smelly feet are often called, 'cheesy'. Research at the Institute of Dermatology reveals that this is caused by an organism called *Brevibacterium epidermis*, which thrives on the proteins in skin in the damp and enclosed space inside a sock. It breaks them down to *methanethiol* ($CH_3 SH$), which produces the smell.

Its close cousin, *Brevibacterium lineus* is added by the makers of Brie and Camembert cheeses, producing a similar smell.

Welsh men and women have the smallest feet in Britain, according to a 1986 survey conducted by a Nottingham boot manufacturer. The survey also discovered that fishermen, farmers, basketball players, policemen, wrestlers and guardsmen wear the biggest boots.

DEAF IN ONE LEG

A London hospital 'lost' a Channel Tunnel construction worker who is still walking around with his right ear sewn onto his thigh. The man's ear was bitten off in a fight; surgeons stitched it onto the inside of his leg, to maintain the blood supply. The surgeon responsible said there was no reason why the ear shouldn't stay on the man's thigh indefinitely, if he liked it there.

BIONIC GRANNY

Rose Iacona from the town of Union, New Jersey, USA was probably the first person in the world to have all her major joints replaced with artificial implants. Fifteen operations over a six-year period were required to replace ten major joints – her hips, shoulders, elbows and knees.

Rose, who at one stage in her life was bedridden, in constant pain and unable to move even to brush her teeth, was last reported to be 'semi-synthetic' but completely free of pain.

ELEPHANTS

African elephants are the world's largest land mammals, weighing up to 6.5 tons and standing up to 3.9 m (13 ft) tall at the shoulder. Their tusks hold the record as the largest teeth of any animal. The heaviest single tusk was more than three metres (10 ft) long and weighed 117 kg (258 lb) – more than a heavy-weight boxer.

Elephants are the only animals with four knees. They purr like cats, can detect water underground and make pillows to rest their heads on when they go to sleep.

An elephant's average body temperature is 39.9 °C (103.8 °F). It breathes twelve times a minute. Its heart, which beats forty times a minute, weighs 12 kg (26 ½ lb). Its life expectancy in the wild is about thirty to forty years if it escapes poachers.

In 1930, Africa held an estimated five to ten million elephants; by 1989 they were on the endangered list with just 600,000 left on the continent, down from 1.3 million a decade earlier. At the turn of the century, Asian elephants numbered perhaps 200,000; today there may be no more than 54,000 left.

In 1992, a world-wide ban on the ivory trade was announced. Since then, African elephants have increased in number again so dramatically, wildlife managers are considering injecting female elephants with some contraceptive agent to stop them reproducing so much. Too many elephants will destroy the natural habitat.

Elephants have frequent colds, but sneeze rarely. An elephant's sneeze has been compared to 'the bursting of a boiler of considerable size'.

The trunk of an elephant is a muscular, but delicate extension of its upper lip and nose combined. It contains some 40,000 muscles and can tear a tree up by its roots. Its sense of smell is so acute, it can sniff water three miles away and other elephants two miles away.

The tip of the trunk ends in one (Asian) or two (African) finger-like projections which elephants can use with great delicacy. They can pick a pin off the ground, unbolt a gate, pull the trigger of a gun, untie a slip knot or, in the case of an elephant kept by the Duke of Devonshire in the 1880s, uncork a bottle of wine.

It is a myth that elephants are afraid of mice but they are afraid of rabbits and Dachshunds.

Elephants need to drink about 75.7 litres (20 gals) of water a day. They spend eighteen to twenty hours a day feeding.

Evidence for the existence of elephant graveyards – secret cemeteries where the great beasts go to die – is thin. Occasionally elephants die together in large numbers due to drought, bush fires or other natural causes and this may have given rise to the legends.

In recent years, researchers have discovered that elephants communicate with each other by producing sounds at such a low frequency that the human ear is incapable of detecting them.

According to observations in the Tsavo game park in Africa, a young elephant will produce 3.6 kg (8 lb) of dung every time it defecates, a large one up to 27.2 kg (60 lb) – an action it repeats fifteen or sixteen times a day, a total of 408 kg (900 lb). Multiply this by 30,000 elephants and you'll get some idea of the amazing job dung beetles have to deal with.

DINOSAURS

Dinosaurs lived on the earth for 165 million years, from about 230 million to 65 million years ago. Palaeontologists have now identified 350 species of which more than half have been discovered only in the last 20 years. There remains much to learn. Scientists believe this number represents only a small fraction of the dinosaur species that existed, all of which probably evolved from a small, nimble two-legged pheasant-size reptile. The first fossils of the most primitive dinosaur yet discovered – known as *Eoraptor* – were found in Argentina in 1992.

The longest dinosaur ever discovered is being gradually unearthed from a desert hillside in New Mexico. Named seismosaurus, it has the long neck and tail of a diplodocus or brontosaurus but is twice as long.

In recent years the Gobi desert has again become a Mecca for dinosaur hunters. Closed to Western scientists for many years, it is now considered the last great dinosaur graveyard in the world. More than forty different species have been discovered here, all dating from the Cretaceous Period (between 135 and 65 million years ago). The only country where more species have been found (about sixty) is the United States.

DINOSAUR EGGS

Few people realise that dinosaurs hatched out of eggs. The first nest of dinosaur eggs was discovered in the Gobi Desert in Mongolia in the 1920s and 1930s by Roy Chapman Andrews in the course of five expeditions to the region.

One of the best sites subsequently discovered for dinosaur eggs is at Montagne St Victoire near Aix-en-Provence in France. Limestone deposits here are almost entirely made up of egg shells and whole nests of a dozen types of egg have been found.

In July 1992, a seventy million year-old dinosaur egg, measuring 18.2 cm (7 ⅛ in) in length (probably laid by a member of the herbivorous dinosaur species *Hypselosaurus*) was auctioned at Christie's in London and fetched £5,500. A similar egg sold at auction in 1972 for £260.

BEARS

Pliny The Elder believed that bears were born as tiny masses of unformed flesh and claws and that the mother bear gradually licked it into the shape of a cub.

All polar bears are left-handed; they never use their right paw in attack or defence. Fully-grown, they can reach 2.7 m (9 ft) tall and weigh 454 kg (1,000 lb). Polar bear livers contain very high concentrations of Vitamin A, an over-

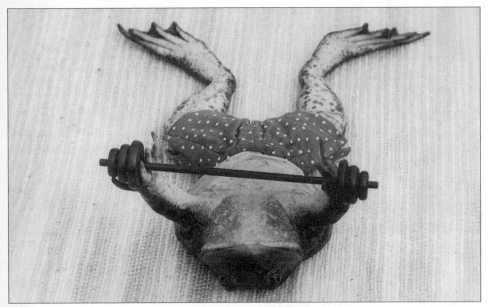

FACT A weight-lifting frog preparing for the amphibian Olympics. In reality, frogs are first hypnotised and then lift the weights lying down.

FACT Dinosaur expert Stuart Baldwin tries to answer the question: which came first, the dinosaur or the egg.

dose of which killed off all the members of a nineteenth century Arctic expedition, who ate the liver of a bear they'd killed

OKAPI

The okapi (*Okapia johnstoni*) has four stomachs, eyes that can look in different directions simultaneously and a 355 mm (14 in) long transparent tongue which it uses to strip leaves from the trees. It has the legs of a zebra, the body of an antelope, the gait of a giraffe, the swiftness of an ostrich and the courage of a tiger.

A horse-like animal, 1.8-2.1 metres (6-7 ft) long, the okapi lives in the dense tropical forests of central Africa. Its brown body with white stripes on the buttocks and legs help to camouflage it and its acute hearing enables it to avoid humans. As a result, it was not sighted by Western zoologists until the last decade of the nineteenth century and not formally identified until 1901.

Okapis lead a solitary existence, coming together only to mate. Afterwards the female goes off alone to give birth.

BISON

The virtual extinction of the bison in the US has become a legend. It was in 1871 that tanners discovered that bison hides made magnificent leather. In just two years, more than 1.3 million hides were shipped East from just two railheads in Kansas. By the middle of the 1880s, bison had virtually disappeared from the American plains.

Farmer Colin Ellis has a herd of thirty bison on his farm near Milton Abbas in Dorset; there are about 170 of these animals in Britain in total. Farmer Ellis saw Walt Disney's movie, *The Vanishing Prairie* when he was a kid and became hooked on these giant, shaggy beasts.

PRIZE CATTLE

A breeder set a new world-record in August 1992 by selling his prize-winning pedigree Holstein Friesian cow at auction for £68,150.

The cow, named Grantchester Heather the Eighth, produces eight to twelve gallons of milk a day and has given birth to four artificially-inseminated calves.

In 1990, the Cantabrian regional government in northern Spain spent 187 million pesetas (£1,075,000) on Sabastian, Europe's most expensive stud bull. Weighing in at 1,100 kg (2,425 lb), this Canadian-born Friesian has certainly justified the investment. In the two years since, Sabastian has sired more than 100,000 calves.

Stock improvement is very big business. Sabastian produces nearly 4,500 doses of sperm a month, valued at 8,000 pesetas (£46) a dose.

FAINTING GOATS

A special breed of goat that falls over in a faint if startled is becoming popular as a farm animal and as a pet in America's Mid-West. A Fainting Goat Association has been established in Iowa; photographic proof of a comatose goat is necessary to achieve membership.

The goats suffer from a genetic defect known as myatonia, which causes their muscles to stiffen when scared. Their average size ranges from 43-63 cm (17-25 in) and they weigh from 18-34 kg (40-74 lb). Distinctive characteristics of these goats are long ears, which stick straight out from the sides of their heads, and bulgy eyes. The goats, which faint for about fifteen seconds, are registered in three categories: premium fainters, standard fainters and breeders.

It is believed that these animals originate from a family of goats brought to Marshall County, Tennessee in the late 1880s by a traveller from Nova Scotia.

No-one knows where he came from or where he went – but he sold his goats to a man named Goode, who then sold them to a certain Dr H.H. Mayberry. Dr Mayberry is credited with saving the breed from extinction.

Farmers would put a goat amongst their sheep so that, if a wolf or coyote attacked the flock, the sheep would flee and the fainting goat would be eaten.

PIG WAR

In November 1974, a full-scale tribal war broke out in the Papua-New Guinea highlands over the ownership of a pig – a traditional symbol of wealth and prestige. During four days of fierce fighting between 2,200 tribesmen from the Yani and Gomgali clans in the Chimbu district, four warriors died and sixty were injured. In addition, 200 houses and many acres of crops were destroyed. Riot police fired twenty-five rounds of tear-gas before they were able to stop the fighting and arrest seventy men.

KILLER BEES

The subject of two B-movies (joke), killer bees are a reality. The phenomenon dates from 1957 when thirty-five queen bees from Africa were introduced to Brazil by Professor Warwick E. Kerr, a bee geneticist at the University of Sao Paulo, who hoped to breed better honey producers by cross-breeding them with Brazil's milder-tempered European honeybee, to whom they are closely related.

African bees are notorious for swarming so Professor Kerr placed excluders in the hives, which allowed the worker bees to get through but not the queens. In his absence, a well-meaning beekeeper removed the excluders and as a result, twenty-six colonies swarmed.

The bees soon proved more adept at viciously defending their hives and genetically overwhelming the country's existing bees than making honey. Hybrid 'Africanized' colonies developed all over the country and the scare stories began.

The bees were first dubbed 'killers' after 300 Brazilians were stung to death in early attacks. Between 1975 and 1988 an estimated 350 Venezuelans were killed by the bees.

In one incident, in August 1973, thousands of the bees terrorised the town of Goiana for hours. The 13,000 inhabitants had to barricade themselves in their homes when swarms attacked two schools and the local market. Firemen clad in asbestos suits used flame-throwers to wipe out the bees. About two hundred people were treated for stings.

The sting of an Africanized bee is no worse than that of the more tranquil European bee but they are very defensive of their nests and attack in large numbers.

According to Dr Thomas Rinderer of the US Dept of Agriculture, 'Even a slight noise, such as a lawn-mower engine or a series of shouts, can set them off. Once disturbed, a colony can remain jumpy for hours or even days.'

Biologist Mark Winston, author of a recent book on the subject, recounts his experience when he first came into contact with the bees in Surinam in 1977:

'Merely walking toward the colonies elicited a massive response on the part of the bees, so that the situation was out of control before we smoked and opened our first colony. Bees were everywhere, banging into our veils and helmets with such ferocity that we could scarcely hear each other.'

Winston was wearing a head-to-toe bee suit over two layers of clothing, boots and a helmet. Despite this protection, he was stung more than fifty times in a few minutes.

Africanized bees have gradually been spreading north, at the rate of 322 km (200 miles) a year, through Central America into the southern states of the US.

In 1985 the first colonies discovered in the US were 240 km (150 miles) north of Los Angeles. They were disturbed by an oil-field worker who saw them

 Apiarist Mark Klaiber of Connnecticut has grown a very unusual bee–ard. He claimed the bees were very docile and he had only been stung once.

attack and kill a rabbit. As a result of this sighting, an area of 1,196 sq km (462 sq miles) was quarantined while scientists searched for the bees, and a state-wide survey of the 600,000 commercial hives – used to pollinate almond, melon and plum crops – was set in train. The emergency was called off after twelve swarms had been located and destroyed. There were no human fatalities.

This was considered an advance group of the main swarms, who made their first appearance near Hidalgo in Texas in October 1990. The first serious attack came in September 1991, when 65 year-old Adan Garza was stung 300 times.

Experience shows that, every time the killer bees reach a new country, honey production drops by at least a fifth. When killer bees begin breeding with European honeybees, the number of beekeepers drops, due to the difficulty of handling the hybrids and because of complaints from the public about being stung.

It's predicted that, for a few years at least, the bees will kill more Americans than all the other poisonous insects and reptiles, not to mention sharks and grizzly bears, combined.

Official advice is that if you do disturb one of these bee colonies, run as fast as possible, downwind (to prevent the bees following your scent) and get into a vehicle or a building. Fast.

CANE TOADS

In the 1930s, Australian agricultural scientists had the bright idea of introducing one hundred Hawaiian cane toads (*Bufo marinus*) into northern Queensland to control the grey-back beetle, the main pest of the sugar cane crop.

The first mistake was that the insects could fly and the toads couldn't so the insects stayed out of reach. Secondly, the toads were more interested in eating other animals than the insects they were supposed to eat. Thirdly, the cane toads were keener on reproducing themselves than destroying insects.

Pesticides had to be used to kill the beetles, leaving behind an even greater menace – the cane toads.

These large, plump, greenish-yellow toads have now established an ecological niche in a country which has no native toads and they are spreading across Australia at the rate of thirty- five km (22 miles) a year.

Cane toads are prolific breeders, they eat anything they can swallow, and highly toxic poison glands behind their eyes, in their skin and in the rest of their bodies make them immune to most predators. Only some species of birds have learnt to kill the toads – by flipping them on their backs and eating their tongues. Cane toads have driven-out indigenous amphibians and poisoned other wildlife and pets.

Rumours spread that drug users had taken to licking the backs of toads, or boiling up their skins, as their secretions contain a substance called, 'bufotenine', which experiments have shown produces hallucinations. The rumour is not matched by fact; only a few people have tried it – and they've been hospitalised as a result. However, dogs have become compulsive toad lickers, as it gives them a kick like alcohol.

In a desperate attempt to control the toads' spread, farmers have organised 'toad eradication' outings, using golf clubs and cricket bats. They have discovered that there may be a market for toad leather. A book, bound in tanned toad-skin was given to Charles and Di on the occasion of their wedding.

The largest cane toad discovered to date is a female nicknamed, Big Bette which is now stuffed and sits in Queensland Museum. It weighs 1.3 kg (2.9 lb) and is twenty-two cm (8 ½ in) long.

Not everyone hates the toads. Some little girls keep them as pets, dressing them up in little frocks and putting them in little beds.

LEECHES

There are some 650 species of leeches world-wide, the largest being the Amazonian leech (*Helobdella ghilianii*) which grows up to 46 cm (18 in) in length. They are in a class of animals called *annelids* and are closely related to the earthworm.

Leeches are most abundant in northern Europe and North America. They thrive not just in swamps but also in Alpine lakes, desert watering holes and polar oceans.

Most leeches don't feed on people or mammals and many of them don't even suck blood. The commonest varieties in a typical freshwater pond feed on invertebrates. Some with jaws eat whole midges, worms or even other leeches. Some have a proboscis like a straw which they use to suck out the soft tissue of snails and mosquito larvae.

About one-fifth of all leeches live in salt water; some of these feed on octopuses. Some live in caves and feed on bats; some can penetrate the skin of an elephant or hippo. Crocodiles get them in their mouths and have birds that come and pick them off their teeth. Ducks get them in their throats and nasal passages, something that is not uncommon among humans in Central Africa.

MEDICINAL LEECHES

The idea of using leeches in medicine was based on the belief that disease was caused by an excess of 'corrupt' blood or by an imbalance in the bodily humours. The Greeks were using them back in the second century BC for treating venomous bites, but they may have been used much earlier than this in India, where they were only used for women and 'timid persons' and for delicate parts of the body.

The medicinal leech has jaws that look like the blades of a circular saw, each with sixty to one hundred teeth, which open the wound in three directions, producing a bite that resembles the hood ornament on a Mercedes.

It secretes an anticoagulant called hirudin which works mainly to keep its meal liquid during digestion. Its saliva contains an anaesthetic which numbs the wound and an enzyme in its saliva slackens the blood vessels.

The leech consumes five to ten times its weight in blood during a half-hour feeding session; the wound it creates bleeds for hours afterwards.

The heyday of medicinal leeches (*Hirudo medicinalis*) was around 1820-1850. The leading advocate was a French doctor, Francois Broussais who once treated his own indigestion with repeated applications of fifty to sixty leeches. An author of the time estimated that leeches were purging 363,000 litres (96,000 gals) of French blood a year. Their use was so common that doctors became widely known as 'leeches' both in the literal sense and in the sense of sucking patients dry of money.

Leech gatherers would simply walk around in a pond with their legs bared and could catch as many as 2,500 a day. So many were caught that the leech almost became extinct and both the French and the Germans had to start leech farming to meet the demand. They also went on leech-buying expeditions into eastern Europe. The Russian government was forced to apply an export ban and a closed season on leech gathering. The medicinal leech remains threatened in Europe today, due to the loss of its swampy habitat.

The main source of most leeches used in modern medicine and research is a company called Biopharm in Swansea, Wales, where a disused steel plant has been turned into a kind of leech-ranch, where more than 50,000 leeches of eight different species are reared at any one time. Every year it ships about 25,000 leeches to researchers in two dozen countries.

Today, leeches are used in microsurgery to help keep the blood flowing while veins heal after surgical grafts. They also provide an animal model for medical researchers seeking to understand how the nervous system works.

In addition, leeches produce a number of biochemicals that are being studied in the hope that they may be useful in the treatment of human circulatory disorders such as thrombosis.

BAT BOMBS

In 1942 the US Army Air Corps captured two million bats and researchers studied how to equip them with delayed explosives. They planned to fix a bomb weighing less than 28 gm (1oz) to each bat by surgically attaching a piece of string to its chest. The bats would then be released over enemy cities where it was hoped that they would fly into attics and under eaves and wait for the delayed fuses to ignite.

The first problem was that the bats kept chewing through the strings. Finally, after two years of research, a trial-run was staged in the Carlsbad Caverns. On the first day some bats escaped and set off fires which destroyed a general's car and a two million-dollar hangar. As a result, the Army project was cancelled.

The Navy then took up the project and tried a new approach. Their theory was that if the bats were artificially cooled, they would be forced into hibernation and so wouldn't chew through the string immediately. The hibernating bats were crated-up and flown to New Mexico where they were dropped from an aeroplane at a great height. The theory here was that, as they came into contact with the warmer air over the desert, the bats would wake up. Official reports reveal that 'most slept on' and fell to their deaths. The project was finally scrapped in August 1944.

THE HERO SHREW

The hero shrew has an unusual spine with bony knobs on it that are designed to prevent the animal from being crushed when it burrows under rocks and boulders. So strong is this backbone that the tiny animal is said to be able to bear the weight of a 77 kg (170 lb) man and survive the ordeal without injury.

THE JUMPING FLEA

Everyone knows that the flea has one of the most remarkable jumps in the animal kingdom. But how does it achieve it ? The answer lies in a special, rubbery protein called resilin, contained in its jumping muscles. A flea can reach its take-off velocity of one metre (3 ft 3 in) per second in a mere 0.8 milliseconds. It contracts its muscles slowly, using them to strain blocks of resilin in a catapult mechanism. Its leap is the elastic recoil of the resilin.

FLIES

Citizens of the Chinese capital of Beijing are being given training courses in ways of wiping out flies. City officials are bidding to stage the Olympic Games in the year 2000 and aim to make the capital fly-free within two years.

Flies can get athlete's foot.

DOGS

In 1986, the premier was held in Amsterdam of an unusual theatrical production, entitled *Going to the Dogs*. The cast of six were all Alsatians.

The man behind the production, Wim Schippers, commented: 'The difference between people on stage and dogs, is that people act while dogs remain normal. Thinking about that gives you a new perspective on the theatre.'

The newspaper, *Leninskoya Znamya* reported in 1976 that the first grooming salon for dogs in the Soviet Union had opened in Moscow.

A San Francisco dentist, Dr Ursula Dietrich, invented a toothpaste for dogs. Called, *Doggydent* - it tastes of beef.

Kathy Coon, a psychologist from Baton Rouge in Louisiana, has developed an IQ test manual for dogs.

There are 53.3 million dogs in America.

Someone has calculated that the dog population in the UK deposits 984 tonnes of excrement and produces 4. 5 million litres (one million gallons) of urine every day. If all that urine were petrol, you could drive the average family car for 4,780,000 km (29,700,000 miles).

Stan, the first dog in Spain to wear contact lenses, was knocked down by a car and killed the day after the fitting, while crossing a road near Bilbao.

In July 1978, an elderly woman in Johannesburg, South Africa, was seriously injured when she was struck on the head by a falling dog. The animal, a miniature Pomeranian, had been thrown from the top of a thirteen-storey building by vandals.

Caliph, a Great Dane, won a place in British legal history when he bit the hand of a judge while on trial for his life – for biting.

On 20 March 1981, the *Times* reported that a dog was struck a glancing blow by a car at a road junction in Sheffield. The driver stopped. The dog picked itself up, ran to the car, jumped up and bit the passenger through the open window.

RIN TIN TIN

Rin Tin Tin earned some $44,000 a picture and died, aged fourteen in the arms of Jean Harlow, after appearing in fifty films.

Found abandoned as a puppy in a front-line trench in France during World War 1, he was known to the enemies of Warner Brothers as 'the mortgage lifter' for his service to the company.

In 1976 the estate of Rin Tin Tin filed suit against film-maker Michael Winner, claiming that his movie *Won Ton Ton, the Dog That Saved Hollywood*, was based on RTT's life story. Winner commented at the time: 'It's absurd to be sued by a dog, especially by a dog who's been dead for the past twenty years.'

DOG-GONE

Dog-Gone is the name of a device like a vacuum cleaner, that removes prairie dogs from their burrows without killing them. Getting rid of these rodents is necessary because they often cause serious damage to cattle ranges in the US Mid-West.

Their removal has traditionally been carried out by killing them in large numbers. This new device will allow the shaken and stirred prairie dogs to be transported to land where they will not interfere with humans – or vice versa. If there is nowhere to relocate them, then the inventor plans to try and sell them in Japan as pets.

HYENAS

Aristotle said that hyenas lured dogs to their deaths by imitating the sound of a man vomiting. Bartholomew, a sixteenth century writer, said hyenas approached houses at night and mimicked the human voice, even calling the people by name so as to lure them out and devour them.

In Africa, hyenas were widely regarded as one of the disguises used by magicians and sorcerers. Magicians in Abyssinia were reported to have turned themselves into hyenas in full view of many people. A story from the Sudan tells how a soldier who shot a hyena followed its trail of blood to a hut, where he found a magician, dying from a fresh wound.

WILD CATS

Modern cats began evolving ten million years ago and have now evolved, due to climate changes and isolation, into a broad family of thirty- seven or so species, divided into two main genera. These are the ten species of big cat that make up the *Panthera* genera (those that roar) and *Felis*, the genera of smaller ones that can only scream or purr.

Each has specializations imposed by its environment. The claws of Canadian lynxes are encased in wide, furry pads that act like snow-shoes; the cheetah, by contrast uses its extended claws as running spikes, enabling it to reach speeds of ninety miles per hour.

In Her Majesty's Dockyard at Plymouth, there is a feral population of 'domestic' cats that may have been isolated within the dockyard walls for 200 years.

The Old World Wildcat, *Felis sylvestris* is the source of all the genes in today's domestic cat. The earliest evidence of domestication comes from an eight thousand year- old jawbone, discovered on the wild-cat-free island of Cyprus. Ships spread the cats (and rats) world-wide.

The Scottish wild cat is the only formidable wild animal remaining in Britain. Dr Terry Moore of the Cat Survival Trust, who has looked after more than 200 endangered cat species suffered an unprovoked attack by a male of the species – it launched itself at his face and clung on 'for what seemed like twenty minutes'.

Dr Moore says: 'The wild cat is notoriously unpredictable and dangerous. At times its behaviour implies it is just mentally unstable.'

BIRDS

In one of the most terrifying bird attacks on record, Italian glider pilot

 FACT A Turkish Van cat is very happy swimming. The stroke it uses is a more graceful style of the doggy paddle.

FACT A member of a rescue team at a British coal mine in full gear, holding a caged linnet, a close relative of the more commonly-used canary.

Antonio Beozzi fought for his life, with a golden eagle, 1,372 m (4,500 ft) above the Alps. The bird swooped straight at the glider and crashed through the cabin cover. Said Beozzi: 'The eagle tore at me. I felt his claws in my flesh. I fought back, covered with blood.' He managed to strangle the bird to death just as his craft dived out of control. He claimed later: 'It was the ultimate fear.'

The navigational abilities of birds are known to be extraordinary but few can compare with the uncanny accuracy of the Manx shearwater, a seabird that was taken to Boston in the US, from its home in Wales. It flew the 4,800 km (2,893 miles) back to its nest in just twelve days, arriving before the letter that announced its departure.

Flemish artist, Roelandt Savery, the only painter who is believed to have sketched a live dodo bird (which became extinct in 1681), painted two right legs on the creature. It became the model for generations of copyists, who repeated the structural error.

POISONOUS BIRD

The first poisonous bird ever discovered by Western science was found in the jungles of New Guinea by a scientist from the University of Chicago – by accident – in 1992.

The bird is called the hooded pitohui, (pronounced *pit-a-hooey*). Its skin and its brilliant orange and black feathers are highly poisonous. They contain one of the most toxic natural substances, a chemical named, *homobatrachotoxin*.

The scientist who discovered this did so at first hand, when several pitohuis got caught in nets he'd set to catch another species. His hands got cut by the birds' sharp beaks and claws and swelled up as a result of the poison.

THE SONG OF THE HUIA

Using a computer, ornithologist and composer David Hindley has recreated the song of a bird that became extinct more than eighty years ago.

Huia birds, (stuffed examples of which can be seen in the Royal Albert Memorial Museum in Exeter) were unique in that the male and female of the species had different shaped bills. The male's stout bill was useful for tearing the bark from trees; the female's long, slender bill was ideally suited for poking out grubs. Thus co-operation between the sexes was vital for survival.

These birds, which lived in the forest of New Zealand's North Island until hunting, habitat destruction and predators finished them off in 1907, had a strange and lovely call. No recordings of the actual call existed but there were three recordings of people whistling an imitation of it. Using these and notations of the huia's call in sheet music form, together with studies of the calls of other New Zealand forest birds like the shining cuckoo and the tui, Hindley created his reconstruction. No-one knows how accurate it is but the eerie and melancholy sound is now available on record.

TURKEYS

A native bird of the North American continent, the turkey was called 'Indian Bird' by the French and renamed, 'turkey' by British settlers, because its profile resembled a map of the old Ottoman empire.

In 1953, the Turkish delegate to the United Nations said that, in his country, turkeys were called 'American birds'.

The big annual event in the Ozark hill-town of Yellville, Arkansas is the 'Turkey Drop'. Seventeen turkeys are flung out of aeroplanes and then hunted down by spectators.

One year, after protests by the Arkansas Humane Organisation, frozen turkeys were used instead. One demolished someone's front porch and another dented a car.

MISSING BUDGIES

Britain's only Missing Budgie Bureau was founded in 1956 in Hartlepool, by Alan Moon, secretary of the local budgerigar society. Since the Bureau was founded, Mr Moon has helped reunite thousands of lost birds with their owners. He advises budgie owners to teach their birds to recite their phone numbers or addresses. One budgie came into his care shouting, 'Hawway the lads. Hawway the lads.' The owners were not difficult to trace.

CANARY IN THE COAL MINE

The 1954 Mines and Quarry Act made it law that the manager of every coal mine should ensure that 'two small birds for testing for noxious gas' be employed below ground. This law dates back to the days when birds were the only safe way to detect carbon monoxide, a deadly gas because it cannot be smelled by humans. Birds, with their smaller amount of blood and rapid breathing, would succumb to the gas in less than one-tenth of the time it would take to affect a human.

In the 1800s, canaries were first used because their bright yellow plumage stood out in dark places. The birds weren't killed off by their work; they were put inside specially built resuscitators – small boxes that could be flooded with oxygen. Some canaries were revived in this way eight or nine times.

All British Coal mines (that are still operational) have birds which are looked after in special aviaries – even though their job has been taken over by modern electronic equipment, which not only warns of the presence of the gas but also gives an exact reading of the level.

The latest scientific evidence suggests that amphibians – frogs, toads, salamanders and newts, may be the 'canary in the coal mine' for the natural environment. Amphibians have survived every major extinction so far, including that of the dinosaurs, but scientists are now reporting dramatic declines in numbers. No-one is yet sure whether this is a natural fluctuation in population, or evidence of a global problem in the natural environment.

Amphibians are especially susceptible to environmental pollution and change, first because they breathe through their skin and secondly because changes in climate would affect the number of breeding sites.

RAT ATTACK

This report was filed by police officer, Steven Briggs of Fort Lauderdale, Florida after he was called out in October 1977 to deal with a rat in a woman's bathroom:

'The undersigned, while equipped with a night-stick, entered the bathroom. At this time, the rodent was observed and the undersigned attempted to destroy it.

'However, during the course of this officer's action, the animal, due to its size, was able to outmanoeuvre the undersigned. At one point the rodent approached this officer in a very quick manner, and therefore in an attempt to avoid the possibility of being bitten, the undersigned quickly jumped onto the bathroom sink cabinet.

'Meanwhile, the rat managed to jump across from the undersigned, during which time this officer struck at the animal, and as a result, broke his nightstick.

'At that point, the rodent made a spectacular leap across the bathroom and landed on the mirror, which was directly attached to the wall directly next to the undersigned's face.

'Then, in an attempt to escape the possibility of the rat then leaping on this officer's face or shoulders, the undersigned quickly leaned away from the animal, while at the same time attempting to strike it with what remained of his nightstick.

'Unfortunately, the officer lost his balance and fell off the cabinet and landed against the opposite wall of the bathroom. As a result of the fall, the undersigned struck the wall with both his elbows and his head, thus receiving bruises to both of his elbows and, as a result of the blow to the head, the undersigned's front tooth broke.

'At that point, the undersigned requested a backup contact to come to the scene in order to supply the undersigned with an additional nightstick in order to continue the battle. Shortly thereafter, another officer arrived and the rat was destroyed.'

POSTAL ATTACKS

According to official figures, 4,250 British postmen are bitten by dogs every year while delivering the mail, and one bite in five is serious enough to cause the postman to stay off work.

One US postal worker in Sweetwater, Texas, was regularly attacked by Mississippi Kite Hawks, sharp-taloned birds of prey. There was nothing he could do to defend himself because the birds are an endangered species. He took to wearing a hard hat and a welder's mask to work.

BIOMASS

Despite more than 250 years of research, we still do not know how many species of living organisms there are on this planet. Estimates vary widely between three and thirty million.

Scientific efforts to classify life on earth have concentrated mainly on animals with feathers or fur. As a result we know a lot about birds and mammals but much less about the more numerous classes of animals. Only about three to five new bird-species are discovered each year and about twenty mammals, (mainly rodents, bats and shrews).

Scientists know far more about the classification of the stars than the earth's living organisms, as information is scattered among institutions around the world and there is no central database.

Insects make up half the known total of 1.5 million species described to date; by contrast, there only 4,000 mammals are accounted for.

MACROSOUND

Tim Davies is a macro-sound recordist. He records sounds which are not audible to the human ear and which are transmitted through solid material such as stone, wood fibre or plant stalk.

He has recorded the sad sigh of a tree, (the noise of the sinews and fibres heaving against each other) and the sound of a Red Admiral butterfly in its chrysalis.

His sensitive equipment, which took him twenty-five years to develop, enables him to pick up such sounds as the 'twang' made as a spider gently weaves its intricate web and the sawing noise made by leaf-cutting ants as they slice up foliage.

CRYPTOZOOLOGY

Dr Roy P. Mackal, a respected research biologist and associate professor of biochemistry at the University of Chicago, has another interest in life – zoological mysteries.

His studies of extinct, legendary, and previously unknown animals – a study known as cryptozoology – have led him to believe that a 'living dinosaur' known locally as the *Mokele-mbembe*, still exists in the jungles of the Congo in Central Africa. He has staged several expeditions to the area to try and track down the beast but with no success so far.

Detective Constable Steve Ashcroft has spent years of his spare-time investigating whether exotic cats really do roam the British landscape.

Eyewitness accounts run at about fifty a week, nationwide. Real or imagined? There are plenty of reported sightings – the Surrey Puma and the Exmoor

Beast are the best known, but there are also the Hayling Island African Swamp Cat and the Kidderminster Jungle Cat to consider.

The generally-held view on this phenomenon seems to be that the cats do exist and that they are either escapees from zoos and private collections, or animals that were deliberately released into the wild when the 1976 Dangerous Animals Act required all exotic animals to be registered.

ZOOS

Wild beasts were kept in the Tower of London for centuries. Henry I, kept a polar bear there, which was let out, daily on a rope and allowed to swim in the Thames. During the eighteenth century, visitors to the menagerie could either pay three half pence or provide a dog or cat to be fed to the lions.

Henry II shot and killed his entire zoological collection of monkeys, lions, camels and bears with an arquebus.

The word 'zoo' first appeared in a music-hall song in 1867 entitled, *Walking to the Zoo is the O.K. thing to do.*

ANIMAL ACRONYMS

In an agricultural experiment, sheep in the mountains of North Wales were fitted with electronic bleepers so that farmers could trace their movements across the rugged terrain. The device was named, the 'Bangor Orange Position Estimating Equipment for Pastures'.

Methane gas from cow manure was used to fuel gas cookers in 3,500 homes in Chicago in the 1970s. The system was run by the 'Calorific Recovery Anaerobic Process Inc'.

DID YOU KNOW?

In the US state of Ohio there is a law that pets have to carry lights on their tails at night.

One of the strangest wildlife books ever published is *Flattened Fauna: A Field Guide to Common Animals of Roads, Streets and Highways*. Using outline drawings, it tells you how to identify flat, dead things lying in the road.

In May 1987, newspapers reported the case of a thirty-six year old man in Hong Kong who was admitted to hospital after being hit on the head by a tortoise which had fallen from a high-rise building. Police held the tortoise in custody, having failed to find its owner.

Snowy the hamster made a miraculous escape from his cage in his owner's country cottage in the village of Bratton Fleming in North Devon after gnawing on a non-safety match which set light to his bedding and subsequently the whole house.

The local fire officer told reporters: 'I know it sounds ridiculous but the whole story is true. We are now issuing a warning to all hamsters not to play with red-tipped matches or to smoke in bed.'

A shark, found near a cave off Kingston, Jamaica had a bunch of keys, a camera, a pair of trousers and a chest of drawers in its stomach.

The butterfly's eye contains 5,000 lenses and 50,000 nerves.

In the small village of Deshnok, in North Rajasthan is the only temple in India devoted to the worship of rats.

In a country where the average wage is £400 per year and 450 million people live below the poverty line, the *kabas* , or sacred rats of the goddess Karnjii, are fed on gifts of food and milk valued at up to £2,500 per year.

In a south-western Indian village in October 1992, a woman bather left a gold chain on the riverbank. It was swallowed by a frog. The woman's relatives killed and cut-open sixty-eight frogs before the chain was found.

Jeff Weber runs an unusual business in Florida called, 'Preservation Specialities Inc'. He freeze-dries pets.

A tourist official in northern Sweden has discovered a lucrative market in the sale of elk droppings, which he sells for 35 kroner (£3.50) per jar. Emmen Zoo in the Netherlands sells buckets of elephant manure which, it's claimed, could be just what your roses need. The profit from each bucket goes to a foundation that protects elephants in their natural habitat.

The world's largest earwig, which grows up to 76 mm (3 in) long is only found on the South Atlantic island of St Helena.

Although most cats hate getting wet, a rare and eccentric breed of cat, called the Turkish Van or the Van Cat of Turkey actually likes swimming and playing in the rain.

Jose Chema, an animal linguist from northern Spain, has teamed up with a donkey that can predict the movements of the share prices on the Spanish stock market. He discovered that the donkey had a natural ability for problem solving that could readily be applied to predicting the movement of shares. Jose can tell from the waggle of the donkey's ears whether a particular share will go up, down or stay the same. Asked whether it is wrong to exploit a donkey for financial gain, Jose replied: 'as long as she gets her hay she is happy'.

WORLD-WIDE

The latest geological evidence suggests that, every few hundred million years, all the continents congregate into a single land mass, or super continent which then gradually drifts apart again at a rate of a few centimetres a year.

The Earth's core – which is more than half the 12,740 km (8,000 miles) diameter of the entire globe – was only discovered in 1906. It wasn't until the late 1980s that scientists discovered the core has surface features like the earth – but upside down.

The core itself is molten iron, the mantle above it, solid rock, 97-320 km (60-200 miles) thick. In places at the boundary of the two, the core intrudes into the mantle and the crust extends into the core, to form anti-oceans and anti-mountains that resemble features on the earth's surface.

One group of seismologists believes that there is even a kind of geological weather system, driven by the heat exchange between the equatorial and the polar regions of the core. Out of this, iron particles 'rain' down towards the core.

Temperatures in the outer part of the core, 1,200 km (745 miles) from the earth's centre reach those of the sun's surface (5,800 °C/10,500 °F) and pressures exceed a million 'atmospheres' (one atmosphere being about equal to 1 kg per sq cm (14 lb per sq in) of pressure). Magnetic tempests develop from surges in the liquid iron, which flows like water; they can be detected on the surface by measuring the waxing and waning of the earth's magnetic field.

The centre of the earth is closer to New York than New York is to Honolulu.

It took the British Geological Survey forty years of hard work to produce a gravity map for the whole country.

OLDEST ROCK

Chunks of granite some 3.96 billion years old were discovered in 1990 by American geologist, Samuel Bowring, on an island in an unnamed lake, north of Yellowknife, in Canada's Northwest Territories. The chunks of granite are believed to be part of the Earth's first crust.

Following Bowring's announcement of his find, two smart prospectors figured out where the site was from the scanty details supplied, hired a plane to fly up there, and staked out the mineral rights. They have since sold large quantities of the black-and-white granite to the locals as curios.

METALS

Almost all metals are 'primordial': they have neither been created nor destroyed since the beginning of the earth 4.6 billion years ago. They have simply moved from place to place.

La Escondida in Chile contains 1.8 billion tonnes of ore which yield 60 billion pounds of minable copper. In the rest of the earth's crust, copper ore is found in a concentration of fifty-five parts per million; at La Escondida the concentration is 300 times greater than that. The deposit is worth more than sixty billion dollars at 1991 prices.

RED DUST

Dust from the Sahara Desert in North Africa fell on Britain three times in three months in 1987. The red dust is carried by high-level winds for more than 1,930 km (1,200 miles) and the increasing frequency of its appearance, so far afield may be a result of erosion in the soils of the Sahel, a 320-1,125 km (200-700 mile) semi-arid belt on the southern fringes of the desert itself.

There have been seventeen Saharan dust falls reported over the British Isles since 1900; ten of these occurred in the 1980s. In February 1903, an estimated ten million tonnes of Saharan dust fell on Britain.

THE DEAD SEA

The Dead Sea is not 'dead'; its waters swarm with microscopic organisms. Landlocked, it is fed by salt springs and by the Jordan River and is situated 400 metres (1,300 ft) below sea level. The oxygen level there is ten times as rich as at sea level.

The Sea's salts are about ten times more concentrated than the Mediterranean's.

LAKE NYOS

One of the strangest natural disasters of recent times occurred on 21 August 1986, when a cloud of poisonous gas was released from Lake Nyos in the African country of Western Cameroon. More than 1,700 people died as the invisible gas – a cold, suffocating aerosol of carbon dioxide – swept up the valleys. In some villages every living thing died, even the insects. The risk of a similar disaster remains.

SNOW

Is every snowflake different? How different is different? This is impossible to prove and hard to study.

Snow crystals not only come in the form of six-sided stars but also in six-sided plates, hexagonal columns, needles, columns capped with stars, plate-capped columns that look like shirt-studs and many irregular shapes. Their shape depends on the temperature of the clouds in which they are made.

ICE

Three quarters of all the freshwater in the world lies in glaciers, which cover eleven per cent of the earth's land surface. During the Ice Age, they covered thirty per cent.

In 1984, Bloomingdale's, a high-class department store in New York, started selling 100,000 year old-glacial ice from Greenland. A one-kilogram (35-oz) sachet – enough for fifty martinis – sold for seven dollars. Over two hundred and fifty sachets were sold in the first week. The ice, described by the man who had the idea as 'the purest edible substance on earth', melts at half the rate of ordinary ice and cracks pleasantly in the glass due to the compressed air inside it.

ICEBERGS

It is claimed that more than 1,450 cubic kilometres (348 cubic miles) of icebergs are calved from Antarctica every year – equivalent to about half the world's water usage.

About four-fifths of these are calved from the ice shelves that make up thirty per cent of the continent. These are large – sometimes immense – flat-topped tabular bergs. They can measure up to 300 m (1,000 ft) thick.

The record length of time spent tracking one iceberg is eleven years. Scientists can get much valuable information by tracking bergs. Most recently, satellites were used by a US team from the Lamont-Doherty Geological Observatory at Columbia University to plot the path, the speed and rotation of an iceberg they code-named, 'B-9'.

B-9 was 155 km (96 miles) long and 35 km (22 miles) wide) when it started its two-year journey toward disintegration. During that period it covered 1,930 km (1,200 miles) at speeds of up to eight miles per hour.

MESSAGE IN A TRAINER

A cargo of 80,000 Nike trainers fell overboard, into the North Pacific on 27 May 1990. The trainers fell from the *Hansa Carrier* (en-route from South Korea), providing oceanographer, Curtis Ebbesmeyer with a surprising and effective way of mapping the ocean's currents. The five, twelve-metre (40 ft) cargo containers lost overboard, sank but the trainers floated, thanks to their air-cushioned soles.

Ebbesmeyer, based in Seattle in Washington State, put out an all-points alert. Six months to a year later, he retrieved, or received reports of 1,300 of the sneakers, washed ashore on the coast between southern Oregon and the Queen Charlotte Islands (off Canada's British Columbia coast). He mapped the drift of the shoes on computer, to show the pattern of the ocean's currents and compared this with the existing computer model of the Pacific based on historical data.

Unfortunately for beachcombers, the shoes were not tied together, so matching pairs were often widely separated. Oregon's beachcombers held 'swapmeets' to try and match up their odd shoes.

The trainers will continue to provide oceanographers with a way of mapping the mechanisms of the Pacific's currents. Shoes that failed to come ashore

 A grotto in the Antarctic ice, formed by the bridging-over of a crevasse. This famous picture taken at Cape Evans, base camp for Scott's last fatal journey in 1912, shows Scott's ship *Terra Nova* in the background.

were swept back across the Pacific and some beached in Hawaii. The remaining shoes will be carried on to Japan and then back round on a second circle of the ocean.

LIGHTNING STRIKES

According to official statistics from England and Wales, dating from 1800, nearly 1,800 people have been killed by direct lightning strikes. The average number killed each year has, however, fallen dramatically from twenty in the late 1800s, to an average of five since 1960.

The same pattern is repeated in the US. Deaths are down from around three hundred a year in the 1890s to an average of ninety-five per year now.

This decline in casualties can be explained by the change in people's occupations. Nowadays, far fewer people work outdoors on farms, and city dwellers are protected by tall buildings and other structures which attract the lightning first.

Outdoor sporting types – golfers, fell walkers and water sports enthusiasts – are now at most risk.

Ironically, as many as one-quarter of people killed by lightning used trees as shelter. Oaks appear to be hit most often as they are often tall and stand alone. If you are caught in a storm, keep your feet together and crouch as low as possible with your hands on your knees.

In Britain, the chances of being killed by lightning are 200,000 to one – even then, you'd have to stand outside in every thunderstorm to hit Britain for a whole year. Under normal circumstances, the odds go out to about one in four million.

Only a quarter of those people struck by lightning are killed. Many are burnt badly and suffer from shock but recover completely. Whether lightning kills depends on which bodily organs the current passes through.

Golfer Lee Trevino was struck by lightning on the thirteenth green, during a golf tournament in Chicago on 27 June 1975. Lightning flashed off a lake, shot through his golf club and ran up his back. He was thrown in the air and then blacked out; when he regained consciousness, he found it hard to breathe and had no feeling in his left side. For some years afterwards, he continued to get pains in his back, where the lightning had dissolved the lubricant between the discs in his vertebrae.

There are approximately 44,000 thunderstorms and between eight and nine million lightning flashes around the world every day. Put another way, lightning strikes the earth about 100 times a second – a rate of discharge that represents about four billion kilowatts of continuous power.

In the US alone, lightning annually causes about twenty million dollars-worth of property damage; it also starts 10,000 forest fires, which combined destroy some thirty million dollars-worth of timber.

A stroke of 'fossilized lightning' was discovered in a 200 million year-old sandstone formation on a Navajo Indian reservation in Arizona in the 1970s by geologist, Michael Purucker.

The air through which a lightning flash passes – at an estimated 422 million feet per second – is heated to temperatures as high as 30,000 °C (54,000 °F) in one millisecond or less. The expansion of this hot air creates a powerful shock wave that can throw people into the air.

If lightning strikes an object containing moisture, the force can boil it off immediately, causing the object to expand and explode.

This happened in July 1974, when an oak tree exploded in Basildon, Essex

 This 1938 portrait shows the climax of evangelist Irwin A. Monn's sermons, when he stood barefoot on a Tesla coil as millions of volts coursed through his fingertips like lightning.

and killed an eleven year-old schoolgirl.

In 1769 in Italy, lightning struck an ammunition dump at Brescia; three thousand people were killed and one-sixth of the city was destroyed as a result.

In August 1987, nine cricketers were injured and one killed during a match at Isleworth, West London; eleven soccer players suffered injury or shock during a match near Newport, Gwent in Wales on 8 April 1979.

In upper New York State in 1985, a farmer was hit by lightning while driving his tractor; an ambulance was called, but on the way to the hospital, it too was struck by lighting. It crashed and the farmer was killed.

The old saying, 'Lightning never strikes in the same place twice' is untrue. Some buildings can be hit hundreds of times a year.

Certain people have also been struck more than once, the most famous documented example being Park Ranger, Roy Sullivan from Virginia, who was struck seven times and survived.

WINDS

We are all familiar with winds like the mistral and the sirocco but, according to a survey of winds of the world, by Frank H. Forrester, these are just the best-known of hundreds of regional winds. These include: the *elephanta* (a strong wind off the south-west coast of India), the *bad-i-sad-o-bistroz* of Afghanistan (also known as 'The Wind of 120 Days'), the *oe* (a localised whirlwind off the coast of the Faroe Islands), the *whuly* (a violent Antarctic storm, often covering an area, just ninety metres (300 ft) in diameter) and the *zonda* of the Argentinean pampas.

HURRICANES & TYPHOONS

The Florida Labor Day hurricane of 1935 sand-blasted its victims to death. Winds of up to 320 km per hour (200 mph) tore off clothes and skin.

In December 1944, The US Task Force 38 was caught in a typhoon off the Philippines, while refuelling at sea. Three destroyers, 146 aircraft and 790 men were lost.

In 1945, the heavy cruiser, *USS Pittsburgh* had its bows ripped clean off by a hurricane.

EARTHQUAKES

The first earthquake detector was made in 132 AD by Chang Heng, a Chinese astronomer and mathematician.

It consisted of a large bronze pot, around the rim of which were placed a series of dragon's heads, each holding a small bronze ball in its mouth.

When an earthquake struck, it would displace a heavy pendulum inside the pot, this opened one of the dragons' mouths so that the ball tumbled out. The ball fell into the mouth of one of a series of bronze frogs, positioned around the base of the pot. This showed the direction in which the quake had occurred.

Many instances of strange animal behaviour before earthquakes have been recorded.

Cattle left low-lying areas the day before the great, 1964 Alaskan quake covered their fields with a tidal wave. A woman reported that her pet turtle laid an egg (which it had never done before), several hours before a minor tremor in San Francisco in 1977. The turtle ate the egg after the earthquake had struck.

In 1975, Chinese scientists used reports of barnyard animals running in circles, rats and mice emerging from their holes, and dogs whining and bark-

ing all night, to successfully predict an earthquake near Haichin. The resulting evacuation is thought to have saved thousands of lives.

Japanese scientists who have been studying seven catfish for sixteen
years, discovered that the fish consistently become livelier several days before
moderately-strong earthquakes. Ancient folk tales link catfish with earthquakes.
The scientists believe the fish react to weak shifts in the Earth's electrical fields.

In August 1992, residents of three North London tower blocks thought they
were experiencing an earthquake. Subsequent investigation revealed that the
short-lived, inaudible vibrations were generated by the equipment being used
by the band, Madness at their concert in nearby Finsbury Park.

Belgian scientists detected a similar effect in 1987, caused by the rock
band, U2.

The Netherlands experienced its most violent earthquake since 1756, in April
1992. It registered 5.5 to 5.8 on the Richter scale and lasted no more than
thirty seconds. (The Richter scale is used to measure the magnitude of earthquakes. Each unit on the scale is equivalent to 30 times the energy released
by the previous unit.)

There are at least one hundred similar shocks a year world-wide. In 1983,
a 4.7 magnitude earthquake, centred on Liege in Belgium caused forty million pounds-worth of damage.

Peterborough in England was struck by an earthquake, measuring 3.3 on the
Richter scale. Just nine months before this, the first meteorite to be observed
landing in Britain for twenty-two years had struck a garden near the city.

There are usually about 12,000 quakes a year along the San Andreas fault in
California.

An earthquake struck north-western Iran on June 21 1990, causing 40,000

FACT A dramatic view of the volcanic eruption on the Icelandic island of Heimaey, which began on 27 January 1973 and didn't end until July that year. Five thousand inhabitants were forced to leave their homes.

FACT The 1989 San Francisco earthquake pulled down a section of the Oakland Bay Bridge, but a nearby sports stadium, filled with 60,000 people, was almost unaffected.

deaths and an estimated 600 million dollars-worth of property damage. It measured 7.7 magnitude on the Richter scale.

VOLCANOES

There are well over one thousand potentially active volcanoes scattered around the globe – from Scotland to New Zealand and from mountain tops to ocean floors.

Mt Toba in Sumatra erupted 73,500 years ago, firing a billion tons of gas and dust into the stratosphere. It produced so much ash that a layer of dust from the eruption still lies inches-deep over India. It is thought that the explosion darkened the skies so much that it plunged the whole climate back into the last Ice Age.

Among the unique geological features of Australia are boomerang-shaped chains of extinct volcanoes, caused by molten rock rising from hot spots deep within the Earth.

The longest and most extensive volcanic eruptions in recorded history began in 1983, when lava began flowing from Kilauea volcano in Hawaii.

Since then, its lava has covered nearly 100 sq km (40 sq miles) – roughly the area of Manhattan – adding 120 hectares (300 acres) of new land to the island. *Kilauea*, ('rising smoke cloud' in Hawaiian), is the most 'awake' of the five volcanoes that make up the large island of Hawaii. *Kohala* is considered extinct. *Mauna Kea* and *Huallalai* have lain dormant for 4,000 years and 190 years, respectively. *Mauna Loa* last erupted in 1984.

Mauna Kea measures 10,203 m (33,746 ft), from its base on the bottom of the ocean to its tip. That is 1,355 m (44,448 ft) more than Mount Everest, the highest mountain in the world.

AVALANCHES

Three of the worst avalanches ever recorded are:

- ✪ The Alpine avalanches which killed half Hannibal's 38,000-strong army in 218 BC.

- ✪ The worst avalanche ever experienced in the US, which killed 96 people when it buried two, snow-bound trains near Stevens Pass in Washington State in 1910.

- ✪ In 1970, an earthquake-triggered ice slide obliterated the town of Yungay and eleven nearby villages in Peru, killing an estimated 18,000 to 25,000 people.

Avalanches have been used as weapons of war. In December 1916, Austrian and Italian troops were fighting for control of the Dolomite Mountains, which were claimed by both sides. Three days of snow, followed by gale-force winds, packed the snow on the slopes. Fighting resumed after the storm. When both sides noticed that their shellfire was triggering-off avalanches, the gunners began training their fire on the slopes deliberately. The soldiers below were buried in huge numbers. In just two days, an estimated 18,000 men died on both sides.

This technique was the forerunner of modern avalanche control.

The worst avalanche in Britain took place, not in a mountainous part of the country but in the downland of Sussex.

The year 1836 saw the whitest Christmas the county had ever had. Before Christmas it had been mild and muggy, but the weather suddenly changed, bringing huge falls of snow which drifted up to six metres (20 ft) deep in places.

Part of the small town of Lewes is overshadowed by chalk cliffs and it was on the top of these that a huge mass of snow accumulated, threatening a row of seven houses and a timber yard below.

 FACT The deadly white cloud of an avalanche bears down on the lower slopes, burying everything in its smothering embrace.

The first fall from the cliff-top landed in the timber yard. Neighbours pleaded with the forty or so inhabitants of the threatened cottages to leave their dwellings, but to no avail.

When the main fall landed, fifteen people, including babes-in-arms and an eighty year-old man, were buried beneath snow and rubble and many were trapped under collapsed ceilings and roofs. Some were rescued but eight people died.

An eyewitness said it was: 'A scene of awful grandeur. The mass appeared to strike the houses at the base, heaving them upwards, and then breaking over the road; and when the mist of snow, which then enveloped the spot, cleared off, not a vestige of a habitation was to be seen, nothing but an enormous mound of pure white.'

The site is now occupied by The Snowdrop Inn.

THE IKUTA LANDSLIDE

On 11 November 1971, at Ikuta in Japan, a team of government scientists from the Agency of Science and Technology began their investigation into the landslides that plagued the area.

They decided to experiment by using fire hoses to simulate heavy rain on a steep hillside. Journalists and tv crews had been invited to cover the event.

Suddenly, with no warning, the entire overhanging cliff collapsed and a huge wave of mud and boulders slid over the onlookers, before they had time to run.

Fifteen people died and ten were injured. A tv cameraman – true professional – managed to stagger out of the mud with a film of the whole incident, which was shown on Japanese television that night.

TSUNAMIS

The Japanese term *tsunami* ('harbour wave') is the correct name for a 'tidal' wave which is generated, not by the tidal force of the moon, but by under-sea or coastal earthquakes, deep-ocean avalanches or volcanic activity.

In mid-ocean, the distance between the tsunami's crests can be 160 km

(100 miles) but the height of the waves will be no more than 90 cm (3 ft). It is only when it reaches the shore that the wave unleashes its full destructive power.

The most destructive tidal wave in history occurred in 1883, when the volcano, Krakatoa erupted and the entire island collapsed into 250 m (820 ft) of water. A thirty-five metre (115 ft) high tsunami was generated, which killed 36,000 people on the islands of Java and Sumatra.

Almost as destructive was the 25-35 m (82-115 ft) tsunami which hit the coast of Japan in 1896. It smashed more than 100,000 homes and drowned 27,120 people.

Tsunamis create strange by-products. During a 1933 tsunami off Japan, the sea glowed brilliantly at night, an effect believed to be caused by the stimulation of vast numbers of a luminous organism, *Noctiluca miliaris*.

Japanese fishermen have observed that sardines caught during a tsunami have enormously swollen stomachs, caused by swallowing vast numbers of sea bed-dwelling *diatoms* (microscopic single-celled algae), raised to the surface by the disturbance.

It has been suggested that tsunamis were responsible for the Biblical Flood, the parting of the Red Sea and the deluge of the lost continent of Atlantis.

The most thoroughly-investigated tsunami in history occurred in the Pacific Ocean on 1 April 1946. A number of oceanographers who happened to be in the area to observe the Bikini atom bomb test were able to witness the tsunami, first-hand.

The tsunami originated from a magnitude 7.2 earthquake, which had struck Unimak Island in the Aleutians off the Alaskan coast. The wave that was generated wiped out the Scotch Cap lighthouse, killing five men, who were sitting inside – ten metres (32 ft) above sea level. It also destroyed a radio antenna, situated thirty metres (103 ft) above sea level.

The wave travelled 3,620 km (2,250 miles) to Hawaii in four hours and thirty-four minutes, at an average speed of 490 mph. By the time it hit Hilo on the main island of Hawaii, it was more than fourteen metres (45 ft) high. It killed 159 people and caused ten million pounds-worth of property damage. Houses were overturned, railroad tracks and bridges ripped up, coastal highways were buried and beaches were washed away.

After this disaster, a Tsunami Warning System was established, run by the US National Weather Service, with headquarters in Honolulu. Computers, satellites and an ocean-wide network of tide-gauges keep an eye on the ocean. If a tsunami threatens, warnings are issued to all threatened points in the Pacific.

KUDZU

Introduced into the US from Japan in 1876 as part of an ornamental plant exhibition in Philadelphia, the Kudzu vine was subsequently promoted by the Federal government during the Great Depression, as a useful way to slow soil erosion. It has since got completely out of hand.

Its roots can grow up to six metres (20 ft) long and twelve centimetres (5 in) in diameter. Unless the root is killed the plant survives. It can grow forty centimetres (16 in) in a day and as much as thirty metres (100 ft) in a year. It spreads so fast that you can actually watch it grow. The vine now covers an estimated two to seven million acres in thirteen South-eastern states.

Dr Jack Tinga is the University of Georgia, a leading authority on the kudzu, has even received calls from Hollywood producers keen to make a horror movie about the vine. 'It's no joking matter, ' says Tinga, 'if you come across a kudzu, simply drop it and run.'

QUAMASH

In his book on the nineteenth-century botanical explorer David Douglas, author William Morwood writes of the quamash or wild hyacinth: 'A member of the lily family whose edible bulbs provided a staple, starchy food for the Northwest Indians. Douglas, who introduced the large blue flowers to cultivation, described the taste of the cooked tubers as 'much like baked pears', though he complained of the flatulence produced which, on one occasion, nearly blew him out of a Chinook lodge 'by strength of wind.'

WEIRD PLANTS

The Angel Trumpet (*Datura meteloides*) has one of the most sinister of all plant pollination strategies. It appears to guarantee return visits by long-tongued hawk moths to its deep blossoms by producing a nectar that the moth becomes addicted to. Botanists noticed that, after the moths fed, they would become so clumsy they would eventually fall on the ground. When they did manage to fly again, their movements were erratic, as if they were dizzy.

The Umbrella Bamboo (*Thamnocalamus spathaceus*) sleeps a hundred years, to prepare for a brief burst of flowering and the production of seeds that contain the germ of the next generation, and then dies. It last flowered in 1979.

The giant bloom of the Devil's Tongue arum lily (*Amorphallus titanum*), 2.5 m (8 ft) tall, from the jungles of Sumatra, attracts large carrion beetles to it by generating an overpowering smell – something like rotting fish mixed with burnt sugar. It is a smell that is known to have made men pass out from taking too large a whiff.

JIMSON

The poisonous Jimson weed, a pest for farmers and considered to have narcotic properties by American Indian tribes, digests plutonium, the most radioactive substance on earth.

The plant, a cousin of deadly nightshade, binds the deadly metal in a protein compound and carries it harmlessly in its cells. The radioactive plants can then be ground into a paste and stored more easily for thousands of years if necessary until the radiation decays to a safe level.

TREES

Alan Mitchell is a world expert on trees and has produced the definitive field guide to the trees of Britain and Northern Europe. He has travelled the length and breadth of this country measuring more than 40,000 trees for a National Tree Register. Which is when he discovered that some trees were disappearing and reappearing.

Take the Zelkova, a relative of the elm and an enormous tree. The biggest, situated by a house near Hereford, was measured in 1904 . Mitchell found it in 1962 and it had grown to twice its previously recorded size. When he returned to the spot in 1973 the tree wasn't there. There was no sign of a stump, nor of one being removed. He spoke to the gardener who had been there for twenty years. He had never heard of it or seen it.

Mitchell visited Inverary in Scotland on four occasions, with colleagues, looking for big trees. On all these occasions they apparently failed to notice two giant trees – a Stika spruce and a Grand fir, both nearly the size of Nelson's column, despite having walked over the exact spot. Mitchell measured them and recorded them in his notebooks. Next time he visited the place, they had gone again. He can provide no explanation for this strange phenomenon.

Britain imports ninety-two per cent of its timber at a cost of more than three billion pounds, annually.

Britain has only thirty-five native species of tree but no other country seems to have as many growing species as we do. Britain has over 1,500 species (which is more than some continents) and 542 of these can be found in one place – the Westonbirt Arboretum.

In 1970, the Forestry Faculty of the University of British Columbia tried a new technique in tree planting – bombing the land with tree plants. The plants were sown and reared in hard plastic shells, the bottoms of which were scored so the roots could push out. Rocks and stumps proved a handicap to this technique, as did the fact that all the shells finished up at crazy angles. But as tree plants are negatively geotropic, (they grow the right way whatever angle they're placed in the ground), some may have sprouted.

If you picked a branch from a sacred tree in ancient Scandinavia, you were condemned to the following punishment: your navel was cut out and nailed to the trunk of the tree and you were then chased around the tree until your intestines were wrapped about it.

In 1927, a horticultural mission set out from Bombay to investigate reports of a tree that lay down at night and went to sleep. According to a description of the tree published in the *Bombay Chronicle* – it slowly inclined towards the earth after sundown. It lay prone on the earth until midnight. It then began to rise slowly and, at dawn, was once again standing upright.

The cedar and the fig are both mentioned forty-four times in the Bible, the olive thirty-seven times, the palm thirty-one, the oak twenty, and the poplar just once.

The Bolivian thicket tree has sharp spines on its trunk to deter animals from climbing it. The Malayan *Ficus* is cauliflorous, that is it bears stem-less flowers and fruit on its trunk.

The word 'bamboo' is said to come from the Malay word for the sound it makes when it burns. The tallest bamboo species, *Dendrocalamus giganteus*, has stems thirty-six metres (120 ft) tall.

A cork oak must grow for fifteen years before its bark is stripped to produce 'virgin cork'. The process is repeated every eight to ten years, to produce better-quality 'reproduction cork.'

The Kapok tree (*Ceiba pentandra*), a native of the tropical forests of Asia and Africa, has large seed pods packed with floss that is used to fill sleeping bags, padded clothing and life jackets.

The only tree in the world inside the boundary of a first-class cricket ground is a common lime at Kent's County ground. There are a set of special rules taking account of its presence: if the ball hits the tree, the batsman scores four runs; if it clears the tree, six runs. A batsman cannot be caught off the tree.

A thirty-metre (99 ft) American elm in the prairies of Kansas has been officially declared a one-tree state forest.

A pine tree on the campus of the University of Florida is the only tree grown from a hundred seeds taken to the moon and back on the second *Apollo* mission. It is planted among a clump of similar pines and not publicly identified.

The Paulownia tree, which originated in Japan but now thrives throughout North and South America, grows at a phenomenal rate – at seven years old it can reach fourteen metres (45 ft) in height and thirty-six centimetres (14 in) in diameter. Its wood can be used for cabinet making and its large, heart-shaped leaves absorb sulphur dioxide, the gas that causes acid rain.

OLDEST ORGANISM

For many years it was believed that the world's oldest living organism was the Bristlecone pine (*Pinus avistata*). Some of the twisted, stunted pines, which grow at the extreme limits of the treeline in the White Mountains of east-central California are 4,900 years old.

Then claims were made for the Creosote bush, a scraggy, slow-growing shrub found in the deserts of California and Arizona. Dr Frank Vasek, an American botanist, was the first to realise that each circular ring of creosote bushes was, in fact, the offspring of one parent plant. The largest cluster he found had a radius of nearly eight metres (26 ft) and was an estimated 11,700 years old. As a seedling it may have been one of the first plant's to grow in California's Mojave Desert.

Another claimant is the Box huckleberry (*Gaylussacia brachycera*), an evergreen shrub that becomes covered with pink flowers in the spring. One specimen, which grows for more than a mile beside the Juniata River in Pennsylvania is estimated to be 13,000 years old.

All these may be beaten by lichens, which grow at a rate of three to fifteen millimetres (1/10 – 1/2 inch) a year. Specimens found in Lapland and Alaska may be at least 9,000 years old but others, discovered in the dry valleys of Antarctica must be at least 10,000 years old and could be considerably older.

MARK TWAIN SEQUOIA

In 1891, A.D. Moore, owner of the largest remaining stand of Sequoias in California, was approached by a man from the American Museum of Natural History who wanted a cross-section from one of these giant trees for display. The tree chosen had been christened 'Mark Twain'- an average member of its species, weighing some 900.000 kg (2 million lb), consisting of 900 cubic metres (32,000 cu ft) of wood, aged about 1,341 years. In other words, it was a sapling at the time Mohammed was born.

The team of lumberjacks cut huge wedges in the tree, chopped out enough wood to build two houses, before toppling it that autumn. Using six-metre (20 ft) crosscut saws, they cut out two sections – one for the American Museum, one for the Natural History Museum in London.

The American slice alone weighed twenty tonnes and was five metres (16 ½ ft) in diameter. It had to be cut into twelve pieces, each weighing 1,500 kg (3,300 lb), to get it down the mountain and onto the railroad cars that transported it to New York.

THE NEEM

For centuries Asian people have been using the leaves of the neem tree (*Azadirachta indica*), a cousin of the mahogany tree, to protect their crops from insect pests, and to make tea and toothpaste.

Now Western scientists have discovered that the leaves contain more than twenty compounds known as 'limoids' which kill insects by mimicking the insect's own hormones.

Some insect pests find the taste of Neem leaves so terrible they would rather starve than eat them.

New insecticides based on the Neem are now being sold, the advantage over conventional pesticides being that they are biodegradable.

Experiments in India suggest that oils derived from the tree are an effective spermicide and substances derived from it may be useful as a male oral contraceptive.

FOREST FIRES

What may have been the largest fire in human history raged on both sides of the Chinese-Soviet border, along the Black Dragon River, from May to early June 1987. It destroyed ten per cent of the world's conifer reserves before it was put out with the help of two Chinese armies.

In 1983 large swathes of the east Kalimantan rain forest in Borneo were destroyed by a fire that environmentalists said was the worst ever. It destroyed more than 28,500 sq km (11,000 sq miles) of forest, valued at more than five billion dollars.

Forest fires in 1988 at Yellowstone National Park and in neighbouring, Western states were the worst in the US this century. An area of forest nearly half the size of Switzerland was burnt out. Some 9,000 fire fighters tackled the flames in a $120 million rescue-bid; the fire claimed seven lives.

The National Park Service's 'let it burn' policy, based on the evidence that fire was a natural part of the park's ecosystem, has been borne out as the natural landscape has regenerated in the intervening years.

The Lodgepole pine, one of the principle trees in Yellowstone, depends on fire for reproduction. The pine's cones require a minimum temperature of 45 °C (115 °F) to open up and release their seeds. The seeds can take advantage of the space, sunlight and nutrients available after a burn.

The annual burning of the Amazon rain forest by homesteaders consumed roughly 320,000 sq km (120,000 sq miles) of rain forest in 1987 alone – an area more than seven times the size of Switzerland. The burning released 1.9 billion tons of carbon dioxide into the atmosphere along with six million tons of dust, soot and smoke.

DODO & CALVARIA

The first known-example of the extinction of an animal resulting in the decline of a plant species was discovered by Dr Temple, an American wildlife ecologist.

The animal is the dodo which lived on the Indian Ocean island of Mauritius until it became extinct in 1681. Dodos fed on the *Calvaria major* tree and, since the birds died, no new Calvaria trees have grown. In 1973 there were only thirteen left, none younger than three hundred years.

The theory holds that the bird and the tree evolved together. The tree's fruit stones have such strong shells that they need to be ground-up and soft-ened by the Dodo's powerful gizzard before they could burst open and ger-minate.

Dr Temple tested this theory by feeding the tree's seeds to turkeys and then planting the softened stones after they had been digested. Three out of ten seeds germinated, and a new Calvaria tree began to grow for the first time in three centuries.

RUBBER

All the natural rubber produced commercially comes from plantations of a sin-gle species of tree – *Hevea brasiliensis*.

In the late nineteenth century, Henry Wickham was paid seventy pounds by the British government to collect 70,000 seeds of *Hevea* from Brazil for Kew Gardens, where they were planted in June 1876.

Whether or not they were smuggled out illegally from the rubber plan-tations of the Amazon basin is an open question. However, the delay in their planting meant that only four per cent of the seeds germinated. These 2,000 seedlings were shipped to various locations in South-East Asia in miniature greenhouses. From those few, three billion trees have grown which produce almost half of the world's natural rubber supply.

TULIPMANIA

Tulips are now part of the national image of Holland but they were first intro-duced to the country in 1550 from Turkey. Wild buds had been growing on the barren steppes and mountain slopes from Greece to Tibet for at least 2,000 years.

A botanist in Leyden named Carolus Clausius experimented with them and traders soon spotted the commercial possibilities, forming the base of what has become an industry which now produces four million bulbs a year of at least 800 varieties.

'Tulipmania' was a curious incident in the flowers' history, which peaked between 1634 and 1637. A rivalry began to develop between growers to produce bizarre and unusual blooms. The result was a speculative market that bubbled out of control.

A nineteenth century account from Beckmann's *History of Inventions* gives a flavour of the mania:

'For a root of that species Viceroy, the after-mentioned articles were agreed to be delivered: 2 lasts of wheat, 4 of rye, 4 fat oxen, 3 fat swine, 12 fat sheep, 2 hogsheads of wine, 4 tuns of beer, 2 tuns of butter, 1,000 lbs of cheese, a complete bed, a suit of clothes, and a silver beaker.'

Beckmann reports: 'At first everyone won and no one lost. Some of the poorest people gained in a few months houses, coaches, and horses, and figured among the wealthiest in the land. In every town some tavern was selected, which served as a change, where high and low traded in flowers, and confirmed their bargains with the most sumptuous entertainments....The whole of this trade was a game at hazard.'

In the end, emergency legislation had to be introduced to control 'Tulipmania' which was throttling the economy and threatening the stability of the government.

Interestingly enough, many of these exotic blooms, which featured prominently in Dutch paintings and Delft tiles of the period, are now known to have been sick tulips produced from diseased bulbs

The cause was the Augustus virus, first isolated in 1947 by Dr Egburtus van Slogteren at Laboratory for Flower Research in Lisse, which he founded during World War 1. Only two Dutch growers out of approximately 10,000 in the country are now permitted to grow these 'diseased' bulbs under controlled conditions.

FANTASTIC ENVIRONMENT!

RAIN FORESTS

Tropical rain forests make up two per cent of the earth's surface and are inhabited by over half the world's plant, animal and insect species.

A study of a twenty-six square kilometre (10 sq ml) area of the Amazon identified 320 species of birds, 800 species of trees and 460 species of butterflies.

Rain forests are currently disappearing at the rate of twenty hectares (50 acres) per minute.

The destruction of rain forests also causes a loss of cultural diversity. In the last century the population of indigenous Indians has fallen from an estimated six to nine million, to fewer than 200,000. Eighty-seven unique tribes have been exterminated in Brazil alone.

★　★　★

SEA & SOIL

Once the fourth-largest inland sea in the world, and the most prolific source of fish in Soviet Central Asia, the Aral is now drying up because of human intervention in the ecological balance.

An estimated 1.2 billion hectares (3 billion acres) – an area larger than India and China together, some eleven per cent of the earth's vegetated surface – has been moderately or severely degraded since 1945.

AIR

Two-thirds of the world's 1.8 billion city dwellers breathe air that contains dangerous levels of sulphur dioxide and dust.

Each person in the US produces an average of twenty tonnes of carbon dioxide each year and one tonne of industrial solid waste every week.

CHEMICALS

The US uses 120 million kilograms (270 million lb) of pesticides on lawns, gardens and trees every year.

More than seven million chemicals are now known and several thousand new ones are discovered or created every year. Some 80,000 are in common use today.

FOSSIL FUELS

Fossil fuels (coal, oil and gas) provide about ninety-five per cent of the commercial energy used in the world economy; their use is growing at the rate of about twenty per cent per decade.

The *Exxon Valdez* oil spill in Alaska's, Prince William Sound covered 7,800 sq km (3,000 sq miles) and contaminated 650 km (400 miles) of shoreline. More than 20,000 birds and 725 sea otters were killed by the spill.

Some five million tonnes a year of the world's total annual oil production – more than one gram per hundred square metres (120 sq yd) of the ocean's surface – ends up in the sea.

The average US car emits its own weight in carbon into the atmosphere each year.

The US throws away enough used motor oil every year to fill 120 supertankers.

ENERGY IN-CREASES

A Russian environment secretary at the UN Office in Geneva has calculated that there are 146 million irons in the Western World (Europe, North America and Australia). Assuming they are used for two hours a week each, they consume an estimated fifteen billion kilowatt-hours of electricity every year – equivalent to half the annual electricity consumption of Greece and a third of Switzerland's.

PAPER

Recycling one ton of paper instead of producing it from virgin wood results in seventy-four per cent less air pollution and thirty-five per cent less water pollution, saves twelve trees, saves more than 2.3 cu m (3 cu yd) of landfill space and 1,440 litres (320 gal) of oil and creates five times more jobs.

European office workers create 3.5 billion sheets of file paper (forty-five sheets each) every day. In addition, there are 800 million sheets of computer print-out, 300 million photocopies made and a hundred million letters written in Europe every day.

WASTE

A Swiss waste-treatment plant has pioneered a process for reducing sewage sludge to odourless dry granules, rich in phosphates, that make an excellent fertilizer. 23,000 litres (5,000 gal) of sludge can, using this process, be reduced thirteen cubic metres (460 cu ft) of granules, which can fit in the back of a small truck.

Sutton Council in south-west London is offering householders wormeries – plastic bins containing up to a thousand tiger worms – to help residents try to save some two million pounds on the local waste disposal bill.

The worms will eat all the organic waste produced by a family of four (except fish and meat scraps), producing compost and a liquid said to be rich in nutrients and good for feeding tomatoes.

The Sewage Bureau of Tokyo had long used waste sludge to make bricks but they are now also using it to make jewellery. The sludge is dried and heated to 1,400 °C (2550 °F) to produce a polished, brown stone.

According to the US Environmental Protection Agency, the population of the US produces enough garbage every year to fill a convoy of ten-tonne rubbish trucks 230,000 km (145,000 miles) long – more than halfway from here to the moon.

US citizens use: a hundred million steel and tin cans every day (recycling only five per cent of them); around forty-one billion glass containers a year (recycling only thirty per cent of them), and dispose of eighteen billion nappies and two billion razors and blades.

WAR

There have been 127 wars and violent internal conflicts since 1945, all but two of them in the developing world.

In 1987, annual military spending in developing countries amounted to $173 billion; in some poor countries, expenditure on arms is two to three times expenditure on education and health.

POPULATION

From the beginning of humanity's appearance on the earth to 1945, it took more than 10,000 generations to reach a world population of one billion people. Now, in the course of one human lifetime, the world population will increase from two to nine billion by the year 2032. It is already more than halfway there.

The world is adding the equivalent of one China's-worth of people every ten years, one Mexico's-worth every year, one New York City's-worth every month and one Chattanooga's-worth every day.

The rate of increase of the world's population has been in decline since it peaked at about two per cent in 1970. Most notably in India and China but in other countries too, birth rates have declined as the death rates of under-fives have fallen.

RICH & POOR

A baby born in a developing country is ten times more likely to die before its first birthday than one born in an industrial nation..

On average, 37,000 children under the age of five die every day from starvation, diarrhoea and easily preventable diseases.

It has been estimated that between 450 and 750 million people are seriously malnourished.

The twenty-four countries of the Organisation for Economic Co-operation and Development (OECD) are; Australia, Austria, Belgium, Canada, Denmark, Finland, France, Germany, Greece, Iceland, Ireland, Italy, Japan, Luxembourg, the Netherlands, New Zealand, Norway, Portugal, Spain, Sweden, Switzerland, Turkey, the UK and the US.

In 1989 these countries had a gross national product (GNP) of fifteen trillion dollars and an average income per head of $17,500.

In the same year, the seven largest OECD economies consumed forty-three per cent of the world's production of fossil fuels, most of the world's production of metals, and a large share of other industrial materials and forest products.

They released approximately forty per cent of global sulphur oxide emissions and fifty-four per cent of nitrogen oxide emissions – the primary sources of acid pollution.

They generated sixty-eight per cent of the world's industrial waste and accounted for thirty-eight per cent of the world's emissions of greenhouse gases.

The combined population of the OECD countries is 849 million; this is just sixteen per cent of the world's population.

Nearly two billion of the world's 5.3 billion people live in poverty. There are also about one billion people who are unable to read or write, over 1.5 billion people without safe drinking water, about a hundred million people who are completely homeless, one billion people suffering from hunger, 150 million children under the age of five who are malnourished, and 12.9 million children each year who die before their fifth birthday.

According to Christian Aid, every £1.50 spent on a jar of coffee in the UK pays only twelve pence in wages and thirty-five pence in production costs to the exporting country. More than half – seventy-eight pence – is taken up by processing, advertising, overheads and profits in the UK.

One Swiss uses as much energy as forty Somalis, and one Russian uses as much energy as one Swiss, unfortunately without getting a decent standard of living out of it.

LIFETIME CONSUMPTION

The average person in Britain consumes the following in their lifetime:

✪ eight cattle, thirty-six sheep, thirty-six pigs, 750 poultry and nearly a tonne of fish.

✪ 8 tonnes of potatoes

✪ 16,761 eggs

✪ 453 kg (996.6 lb) of carrots

✪ 9,286.5 litres (16,341 pints) of milk

✪ 4,907 loaves of bread

✪ 14,571 pints of beer (that's 193 pints a year)

✪ 2,793 toilet rolls

✪ 5,460 packets of crisps

✪ 302 tubes of toothpaste

✪ 5,5828 bars of soap

✪ 36 pots of Marmite (125g – 4 oz)

✪ 8,456 packs of chewing gum

✪ 762 cans of baked beans

✪ 11,544 Smarties

✪ 6.8 g (0.24 oz) of caviar

✪ 8 kg (18 lb) of dirt, due to poorly-washed vegetables.

EARTH SUMMIT

During the twelve days of the 1992 Earth Summit in Rio, where world leaders discussed the future of the planet, environmental groups claim that: 600-900 plant and animal species became extinct, 197,356 hectares (487,200 acres) of arable land turned to desert, the world's population grew by 3.3 million and 534,000 hectares (1.17 million acres) of tropical rain forest were destroyed.

HUMAN SUFFERING INDEX

The 1992 International Human Suffering Index ranks countries on a league table according to factors like clean water, adequate food, and education. The five lowest on the league were Sudan, Haiti, Afghanistan, Somalia and, worst of all, Mozambique. The five countries with the least human suffering were, at Number One, Denmark, followed by Holland, Belgium, Switzerland and Canada. America ranked fifth and Britain twenty-second.

The Index shows that three quarters of the world's people live in countries where human suffering is the rule rather than the exception.

FANTASTIC ODDMENTS!

LIFESTYLES

Waiters cover an average of ninety-six kilometres (sixty miles) during a five-day working week – the equivalent of 2.3 marathons. Postmen clock up fifty kilometres (31 miles) a week, removal men, forty-one kilometres (26 miles), nurses forty kilometres (25 miles), housewives twenty-four to thirty-two kilometres (15-20 miles) and shop assistants, fourteen kilometres (9 miles).

The survey, by a foot-care company, calculates that each time a ten-stone adult takes a step, the foot is subjected to ninety kilograms (200 lb) of impact pressure.

The average man or women spends three years in a lifetime, just waiting. Washing and dressing take up another five years and telephone conversations a year. Six years are spent eating, five years are spent travelling, amusements consume eight years and we are ill for eight years. We look in the mirror for a total of seventy days and spend ten days in total blowing our noses.

According to a report published in the *Journal of the American Psychosomatic Society*, women are more likely to die of natural causes in the week after their birthdays than any other week of the year.

THE CENTRE OF THE WORLD

Jacques-Andre Istel has declared Felicity, California, the Official Centre of the World. Named after his wife Felicia, the town is set in 1,130 hectares (2,800 acres) of desert, fourteen kilometres (9 miles) west of Yuma, Arizona.

Istel wrote a children's book about the idea and had a legal declaration made by the board of supervisors of Imperial County, California. The exact location of the Official Centre is in a specially-built pyramid, which is surrounded by the rest of the town – a restaurant, a store, a few apartments and a train station at which no train yet stops. They also have a section of staircase from the Eiffel Tower.

FRIDGE-FACTS

A Gallup survey of what people in the UK keep in their fridges revealed some surprising facts. For instance, three per cent store live maggots and one per cent fill their fridges with nothing but alcohol. Other surprising fridge-finds include dead budgerigars, frogs and snakes awaiting stuffing, snake bite serum, wilting wedding bouquets, urine samples and car keys.

STRANGE LAWS

In 1987, Representative Pointdexter introduced a bill in the Mississippi legislature to permit dwarfs to hunt deer with crossbows during the archery season. Look out William Tell!

The City Council of Chico in California once banned nuclear weapons. Anyone detonating one within city limits would be fined $500.

In 1987, a Philadelphia Councilman introduced a bill to ban people from carrying snakes in public. He told a city newspaper that he was 'tired' of seeing people carrying snakes in public.

ST JOHN'S AMBULANCE

Few people realise that the St John Ambulance Brigade, a familiar sight at British public functions, is run by the Sovereign Military Hospitaller, Order of St John of Jerusalem, of Rhodes and Malta, the oldest order of chivalry – now transformed into one of the greatest and least publicised charitable organisations in the world.

Founded in 1099 to care for sick pilgrims in the Holy Land, it turned into a military monastic order, aggressive for the Cross. Today it numbers some three thousand knights around the world and has a world fleet of 150 ambulance aircraft.

Recognised diplomatically by forty countries (but not Britain and the USA), its Prince or Grand Master is technically a Head of State.

In October 1989, the first gathering of the Knights of Malta since 1798 took place. It was attended by five hundred members.

SNUFF

Every British MP is entitled to have a pinch of snuff at the House of Commons – courtesy of the British taxpayer. The snuff is kept in an oak-and-silver box at the entrance to the Chamber of the Commons The box is made out of the remnants of an earlier box that was destroyed during wartime bombing. It bears a silver plate with the names of the doorkeepers who have, over the years, offered MPs snuff.

Tribes in the Amazon jungle bind two plovers' bones together to blow snuff up each other's nostrils. So powerful is the snuff, it's known by such names as 'Leaves of the Angel of Death' and lead to violent fits of sneezing followed by vivid hallucinations.

WINKING WRITER

A fifty-five year old Japanese woman, totally paralysed by a rare disease, completed a 280-page book in two years by winking. The wink controlled a cursor on a computer screen, confirming the letter she wanted to use.

OLDEST HUMAN HAIR

The oldest human hair yet found in the Western hemisphere was discovered in 1992 by archaeologists in a cave in New Mexico. It is believed to be 19,000 years old. This is 4,500 years older than previous 'oldest hairs'; three of which were found in Montana in 1986. The hair is half an inch long, and was found alongside 28,000 year old fingerprints.

RISKS

In Britain, a car driver is eighteen times more likely to die in a crash than a passenger on a train.

Every year there are 1.3 deaths per hundred million passenger miles of car travel. This compares with 0.04 for scheduled air transport.

George Armstrong Custer took out a $5,000 life insurance policy shortly before the Battle of the Little Big Horn.

FLU

Common influenza , or flu, has produced ten major and twenty minor pandemics in the last 250 years. It was first described by Hippocrates, the 'father' of Western medicine, who reported a flu epidemic in the Athenian army in 412 BC.

The greatest known flu pandemic lasted fifteen months during 1918-19 and took between twenty and forty million lives – more than all those killed in the four years of World War 1. It infected at least one-fifth of the total human population of the time.

Called 'Spanish flu', it is now believed to have originated in the US where it took 55,000 lives. In San Francisco, over a quarter of the 3,500 patients admitted to one hospital died. In the city's streets, people walked around wearing gauze face masks to protect against infection; the signing of the Armistice was greeted, according to one observer, by 'tens of thousands of deliriously happy, dancing, singing, masked celebrants.'

RABIES

There are two main forms of this disease found in animals and men: the excited or furious form and the paralytic or dumb.

The outstanding symptoms in all cases is hydrophobia, a fear of water. This comes from the painful spasms of the muscles used in swallowing and breathing, spasms induced by attempts to eat and drink.

The victim produces strange hoarse sounds which early authors described as being like the barking of dogs. An authority on tropical medicine writes that 'these spasms are so agonizing that they exceed, possibly, all other forms of human suffering.

The cure for rabies, decreed by law in eighteenth century Ireland, was to smother the patient between two feather beds and then get a 'sufficient number of the neighbours lying on it' still he was out of danger.

YO-YO

Yo-yos may have originated in China, in ancient Greece, or in both. They were used as a weapon in the Philippines and were a favourite toy of the French nobility, at the time of the Revolution. George IV, Louis XVI and Marie Antoinette were all keen yo-yoers.

The modern history of the yo-yo dates back to 1927 when Pedro Flores, a Philippine-born porter at a hotel in Santa Monica in California, began giving impromptu demonstrations of his home-made yo-yos to the guests. This was so successful that he set up his own factory, which was subsequently bought out by Donald F. Duncan of Chicago.

Duncan patented the name and persuaded William Randolph Hearst to promote yo-yos in his newspapers. Mary Pickford, Douglas Fairbanks and Bing Crosby were among the stars who helped turn the yo-yo into a major craze. Three million yo-yos were sold in one month in Pennsylvania alone in the 1930s, making Duncan a very rich man. With his riches he diversified, manufacturing eighty per cent of America's parking meters.

HULA HOOP

One claim for the origin of the hula hoop is that it began with children in the backstreets of Sydney, Australia, who would remove the loops from old casks and spin them with their bodies.

In the 1950s, hula hoops became a twelve million-pound a-year industry. They were promoted, among other things, as slimming aids, but ended up causing an increase in back complaints. They were banned in Japan because they were causing so many traffic accidents.

POGO STICK

Pogo sticks became a craze amongst the upper-crust of Paris in the 1920s,

 FACT The yo–yo, a simple and relaxing hobby that requires just a little manual dexterity, except if you want to be a real show–off.

after an explorer brought back a sketch of a stick used by the Dyaks in Borneo for sacrificial dances. The pogo stick craze boomed again in the 1960s.

GAMES

Board games date back as far as 3,000 BC, the date of one dug out from the Royal Tombs of Ur by Sir Leonard Woolley. This game used a twenty-square board with seven black and seven white counters, and is thought to have been the ancestor of backgammon. An unusual feature was that it was played with six pyramid-shaped dice.

A UN book on Afghan children's games claims that their favourite is called 'Castigation'. The rules of the game are that the person who is 'It' is bound hand a foot, thrown to the ground and kicked until he manages to spit at another player, who then becomes 'It'.

MONOPOLY

Monopoly is the best-selling copyrighted game ever, with sales of around a hundred million sets world-wide.

Invented by Charles Darrow, an unemployed heating engineer from Philadelphia, it was eventually sold to Parker Brothers after they had initially turned it down in 1973, claiming that it contained 'fifty-two fundamental playing errors'. Darrow was able to retire a millionaire at the age of forty-seven on the game's proceeds and spent the rest of his time growing exotic orchids.

The street names on the American version of the game all come from Atlantic City. The Monopoly lobby successfully prevented the Atlantic City council from trying to change one of the city's street names.

The most expensive Monopoly set in the world was made by Alfred Dunhill and cost five thousand dollars.

An edible version of Monopoly featured a board, property cards and player's symbols made of dark chocolate, and hotels and houses made of milk chocolate or butterscotch. The price tag: £300.

In 1977, competitors in the British Monopoly championships wore protective clothing. The event was held above the nuclear reactor pile at the Oldsbury-on-Severn power station near Bristol.

CLUBS & SOCIETIES

The American Tentative Society is a group dedicated to the view that all knowledge is tentative. After ten years, it had four officers, no members and no fixed policy.

The Circuit Riders Motorcycle Club in the USA is entirely made up of motorcycling ministers.

The Guild of the Nineteenth Lubricators is a London-based charitable organisation. It got its name because all the original founders enjoyed the kind of lubrication that came from a bottle of wine.

The 'Old Corporation' of Malmesbury in Wiltshire is a society of 'free men' who own 4-5,000 acres of farmland in the area and thirty to forty properties in the town. The majority of its members are direct descendants of men who helped King Athelstan defeat the Danes in a battle near Malmesbury in the tenth century.

The Sons of the Desert, organised in 'tents' rather than lodges, are all hard-core fans of Laurel and Hardy and take their name from one of the duos most famous films.

CHARITY RUNS

Terry Fox was eighteen when doctors discovered cancer in his right leg and were forced to amputate it. Angry at it his predicament and unable to adjust emotionally to it, Fox set himself an enormous challenge – to run across Canada to raise money for the Cancer Society.

With the aid of an artificial leg, he ran a marathon a day for 5,375 km (3,359 miles) until he was forced to abandon his coast-to-coast attempt at Thunder Bay in Ontario. He died shortly afterwards.

His extraordinary run raised twenty-four million dollars – more than a dollar for every man, woman and child in his country.

In 1985, nineteen-year old Steve Fonyo, who lost his left leg at the age of twelve, ran across Canada – a distance of almost 8,000 km (5,000 miles) – in fourteen months, wearing-out six artificial legs in the process. He raised almost seven million dollars for charity.

CALENDARS

Not everyone keeps time by our 365-day, twelve-month calendar, which is based on the Earth's orbit around the Sun (one year) and the Moon's orbit around the Earth (one month).

The Muslim calendar is based on the phases of the Moon and has twelve months of twenty-nine or thirty days, producing a total of 354 days in a year.

The Balinese have a *saka* year, which lasts for twelve months and a *wuku* year, consisting of 210 days, arranged in one to ten-day weeks. Priests practice the esoteric art of harmonising the two.

Roman Years had only ten months (December comes from the Latin, *decem* meaning ten) and the new year began in March. Late additions were

January and February. Julius Caesar produced the Julian Calendar which, slightly modified by Pope Gregory XIII in the sixteenth century and re-christened, the Gregorian Calendar, is the one most used in the world today.

The only place in the British Isles that celebrates Christmas Day on 6 January is the Shetland Island of Foula, which still adheres to the old Julian calendar. (The Gregorian calendar was adopted by the rest of Britain in 1752).

BIBLES

The Bible, or portions of it, has now been published in 1,783 languages and dialects. The rate of translation has accelerated. It took nearly forty-six years up to 1980, to translate the New Testament into one hundred languages; the 200th translation was complete by 1983.

The United Bible Societies of America and Europe (UBS) now distribute 500 million Bibles a year. Bibles are available in the languages of ninety-seven per cent of the world's people but 2,500-3,000 languages have yet to be tackled.

TEACHERS

Leicester University once held a Golden Pillow contest for the most boring lecturer of the year. The winner was a physicist who spoke on 'classical mechanical formalism for motion in an infinite viscous medium.'

The runner-up, who was awarded a Silver Pillow, lectured on the German vocabulary, particularly words for parts of the leg below the ankle.

Both pillows were stuffed with shredded papers from boring lectures.

The Eton College Chronicle records that Dr John Keats, the headmaster from 1809 to 1839, used his birch twigs a great deal. In 1818, the boys rioted and smashed his desk to pieces with sledge-hammers, but Keats remained unconcerned and carried on teaching among the debris.

The 'greatest of them all' was Dr Heath who, one occasion, flogged seventy boys, one after another. The result was that he 'injured himself so badly that he was laid up with aches and pains for more than a week.'

COLLECTIVE UNCONSCIOUS

An unusual export consultancy service, founded by two Frenchmen, applies the psychiatrist C.G. Jung's ideas of the 'collective unconscious' to the business of international marketing. Their work claims to show that the collection of deeply-rooted notions, prejudices and taboos that lie at the heart of a nation's culture, are a key factor in shaping our response to new ideas and products...

Take attitudes towards pain. In Japan, pain is something to be openly suffered. In Germany it must be kept as a private experience. In both countries it is felt necessary to suffer pain as a necessary part of life, so sales of pain killers are limited.

In the USA, by contrast, pain is an enemy to be killed, an insult to the American way of life. In France, pain is seen as something that is done to you by somebody else, and medicine is regarded as poison.

ACCIDENT-PRONE

There are more than 28,000 accidental deaths in Britain every year and some two million people receive medical treatment annually as a result of accidents.

According to Dr Ian McQueen, author of *The Family Health Encyclopaedia*, 'the rapid development of machinery and the increase in the complexity of living have converted accidents into the major epidemic of the twentieth century.'

A bus-conductor from Peterborough claimed to be the most accident-prone man in Britain. In the five years up to 1981, he had been involved in five car crashes and four bus breakdowns, had fallen into a river, been knocked down by a motorcycle and walked through a plate glass door.

In February 1979, a man from Acton was mugged on a Monday and robbed of all he had. In the middle of that same week his house was burnt down. Then his dog was killed. In an effort to cheer himself up he went drinking and was arrested twice in the same day for being drunk. He told the local magistrates: 'It's been a very bad week for me'; they fined him ten pounds.

Monsieur Baernard Acheiaus suffered seventeen disasters in three years.

His cycle of bad luck began on 20 September 1980 when the Loire burst its banks and flooded acres of his woods. His parked car was then submerged by another flood. A few weeks later it caught fire, after being stolen four times, each time returning more badly damaged than before. As if this were not enough, lorries dumped their entire load on his car bonnet in two separate accidents.

He bought a cement mixer; it was crushed by a car whose driver had lost control. His billiard table was smashed when the removal firm dropped it. At about the same time he suffered his fourteenth bone fracture while playing rugby. Then his chimney and part of his roof blew off. He was taken in by the police for questioning, after a professor committed suicide in the cellar of his shop. The major part of his remaining woods that had not been flooded burnt down.

DID YOU KNOW?

A Chicago census-taker was so enthusiastic about his job that he lost it. He was arrested on a disorderly conduct charge after repeatedly kicking, screaming and banging on people's doors demanding entrance. The police said that if residents did open their doors, the man 'sprang like a gazelle into their living rooms and began pumping them for information.'

When a certain Mrs Cros of Los Angeles won a local competition for Housewife of the Year, she chose to dynamite a bridge as her prize.

Pro basketball player Clifford Ray of California's Golden State Warriors was called in to help retrieve a piece of metal from the stomach of a 160 kg (350 lb) dolphin. Only his one metre (3 ft 3 in)-long arms could reach it.

Police in Winchester, England, received an emergency call from a man whose wife was holding him against his will by hiding his artificial leg.

Colonel Amelio Robles was a hero of the 1910 Mexican revolution and had a brilliant military career spanning sixty-six years. Then he was forced to go into hospital with a serious illness and the doctors discovered that 'he' was a woman.

It turned out that, after she had given birth to a daughter, Amelio had entered the army without going before any recruiting board and had successfully avoided any medical examinations throughout her long career.

After the Battle of Waterloo in 1815, the then Duke of York had a corridor of his home – Oaklands, in Surrey – lined with the teeth of horses killed in the battle.

The Romans were the first to produce glue, by boiling down mistletoe juice and then spreading it out on trees to catch birds. Glue has also been produced from blood, milk, potatoes, and bones.

In Britain, the 3M company has produced more than forty-five million fragrance strips for British magazines and department stores, who include them in statements to account customers.

The landlord of the Red Lion at Liskeard in Cornwall has, at last, found a use for the twenty Zimmer frames left with him by the previous owner of the property. He has fitted them out with bells and reflectors and lets them out to customers who have had one-over-the-eight. His motto: 'Be sloshed, be safe, be seen'.

Northumbrian Water has opened what it claims is England's most scenic loo. The £250,000 lavatories have been built on the banks of Kielder Water, Europe's largest man-made reservoir. The view from the washbasins is 'spectacular' according to the company's recreation manager, Chris Spray.

Dr Jan Lavric was tired out after successfully shepherding a party of disabled people in to an audience with the Pope. He sat down in a spare wheelchair only to find himself being pushed, protesting, into line with his charges. Dr Lavric, a Doncaster GP and a fitness fanatic, kept an embarrassed silence as the Pope walked past and then gave onlookers a shock when he suddenly rose from his chair to explain the mistake.

A BBC cameraman was sent to film an intrepid oystercatcher which had laid its eggs in a nest between the rails on the busy London-to-Holyhead Intercity line. The cameraman rather spoilt matters when he inadvertently stepped on the nest.

Japan has agreed to dig up a tomb containing 20,000 noses of Korean warriors and return them to South Korea for re-burial. The noses were sliced off by Japanese samurai in the sixteenth century as part of a victory ritual.

In 1989, BEI Defence Systems ran a Scratch 'n' Sniff ad. for its Hydra-70 weapons system in *The Armed Forces Journal*. The picture was of two battling helicopters; when the advert was scratched, it gave off the smell of cordite.

A titillomaniac is a compulsive scratcher.

SOURCES

BOOKS

R. McNeill Alexander, *Elastic Mechanisms in Animal Movement* (Cambridge University Press, 1988)

Dorothy Baldwin, *Human Biology and Health* (2nd Edition. Longman, 1985)

The Bathroom Reader's Institute, *Uncle John's Third Bathroom Reader* (St Martin's Press, 1990)

Peggy and Alan Bialovsky, *The Teddy Bear Catalog* (Workman Publishing, 1981

Howard Blum, *Out There* (Simon & Schuster, 1990)

C.V.Boys, *Soap Bubbles* (Dover Books, 1959)

Andrew Brown, *Soccer's Strangest Matches* (Robson Books, 1989)

Lester R. Brown et al, *State of the World 1992* (Earthscan, 1992)

The Brothers Capek, *R.U.R. and The Insect Play* (Oxford University Press, 1973)

John Cassidy, *The Unbelievable Bubble Book* (Klutz Press, California, 1987)

Phillip Clark, *The Soviet Manned Space Program* (Salamander, 1988)

John Stewart Collis, *Living With a Stranger* (VAL Publishing, 1987)

Stanley Coren, *The Left-Hander Syndrome: The Causes and Consequences of Left-handedness* (John Murray, 1992)

James Curley, *Refried News* (Signet, 1992)

Rodney Dale and Joan Gray, *Edwardian Inventions* (W.H.Allen, 1982)

Hermine Demoriane, *The Tightrope Walker* (Secker & Warburg, 1989)

Shakuntala Devi, *Figuring* (Penguin Books, 1992)

The Diagram Group, *The Book of Comparisons* (Sidgwick & Jackson/Penguin Books, 1980)

Did You Know? (Reader's Digest, 1990)

John Elkington, *Sun Traps* (Penguin Books, 1984)

Exploring Space (Scientific American. Special Issue, 1990)

Facts & Fallacies (Reader's Digest, 1988)

David Filkin, *Bodymatters* (BBC Books, 1988)

Martin Gardner, *The Magic Numbers of Dr Matrix* (Prometheus, 1985)

Kenneth Gatland et al, *The Illustrated Encyclopaedia of Space Technology* (Salamander, 1981)

Edward Goldsmith & Nicholas Hildyard (Eds), *The Earth Report 2* (Mitchell Beazley, 1990)

Senator Al Gore, *Earth In The Balance* (Earthscan, 1992)

"Steam Train" Maury Graham and Robert J. Hemming, *Tales of the Iron Road* (Paragon, 1989)

John Grant, *A Book of Numbers* (Ashgrove Press, 1982)

William R. Gray et al, *Powers of Nature* (National Geographic Books, 1978)

Douglas Greenwood, *Who's Buried Where In England* (Constable, 1982)

The Guinness Book of Records (Guinness Books, 1993)

Thomas Harrison, *Fire From Heaven* (Pan Books, 1977)

Gwyn Headley & Wim Meulenkamp, *Follies* (Jonathan Cape, 1990)

Seymour Hersh, *Chemical & Biological Warfare* (McGibbon & Kee, 1968)

Vincent M. Holt, *Why Not Eat Insects ?* (British Musuem (Natural History), Reprinted 1988)

Geoffrey Howard, *Wheelbarrow Across the Sahara* (Grafton, 1992)

Cyril Isenberg, *The Science of Soap Films and Soap Bubbles* (Dover Books, 1992)

Andrew Kitchener, *The Natural History of the Wild Cat* (Christopher Helm/ A & C Black, 1991)